Baskets:
Celtic Style

Baskets:
Celtic Style

by
Scarlett Rose

American Quilter's Society

P. O. Box 3290 • Paducah, KY 42002-3290

Located in Paducah, Kentucky, the American Quilter's Society (AQS), is dedicated to promoting the accomplishments of today's quilters. Through its publications and events, AQS strives to honor today's quiltmakers and their work — and inspire future creativity and innovation in quiltmaking.

EDITOR: ANNE SONNER
TECHNICAL EDITOR: BONNIE K. BROWNING
BOOK DESIGN/ILLUSTRATIONS: ELAINE WILSON AND JUSTIN GREEN
COVER DESIGN: TERRY WILLIAMS
PHOTOGRAPHY: CHARLES R. LYNCH

Library of Congress Cataloging-in-Publication Data
Rose, Scarlett
    Baskets--Celtic style / Scarlett Rose
         p.   cm.
    Includes bibliographical references (p. 157)
    ISBN 0-89145-891-3
    1. Appliqué -- Patterns.   2. Quilting--Patterns.   3. Baskets in art.
4. Decoration and ornament, Celtic.   I. Title.
TT779.R66   1997
746.46'041--dc21   97-32176
                                                      CIP

Additional copies of this book may be ordered from: American Quilter's Society, PO Box 3290, Paducah, KY 42002-3290 @ $19.95. Add $2.00 for postage & handling.

Dedication

FOR MARY ROSS PEARD

A very dear friend
who helps me to see
what is obvious.

Acknowledgments

A special thank you to Betty McFadyen and Lois Love for making samples for this book. Thank you to Rose Marie Straw, Martha Hilbert, Kathy Mattox, Edy Goldsworthy, Roberta McLaughlin, Judy Hafner, Linda Gibbs, Halli Keller, Marci Cohen, Laurie Short, Bonnie Linn, and all the other ladies of the Quilter's Sew-Ciety of Redding. Thanks also to my father Ellis, my brother Vance, his wife Jennifer, and their two girls Ami and Heather, Aunt Bette and Aunt Mary. I would also like to thank: Ed and Myrna Tamm, Al Krch, Kathy Owen, Sandy Halloway, Lois and Lawrence Schuler, Irene D'Amato, Virginia Morelli, Vivian Crowe, Pete and Peggy Hufford, and all the ladies I work with at the fabric store. My life is so much richer because of all these people. And last but not least, my husband, Dan Nobriga!

Contents

Chapter 1 Evolution 8

Chapter 2 Review of Basics 10

Chapter 3 The Quilts. 15

    New Directions — New Beginnings 16

    Interlaced Tracery 22

    Whole Cloth Baskets 32

    Nightmare Medallion 37

    Indian Summer — Changes 42

    Out of Darkness — Hope. 49

    Scarlett's Roses. 58

    Flowering Basket. 64

Chapter 4 More Variations 68

Chapter 5 The Patterns 78

    Section Patterns 78

    Flower Patterns. 110

    Block Patterns 120

    Basket Patterns. 133

Bibliography. 157

Sources 158

About the Author 159

(Metric equivalents are given in parentheses for all yardage measurements.)

Evolution

This book is the next step in my exploration of interlaced designs. These interlaced basket patterns were inspired by my interest in Baltimore album appliqué quilts. These quilts are very beautiful and elaborate. I will probably never make one, but I do admire them. One evening during a discussion with a group of friends, I mentioned that a woven basket of flowers was one of the Baltimore album patterns that I might actually make some day. My friend Mary Peard pointed out to me that these woven baskets could be easily adapted to my style of interlaced scrollwork. The idea had never occurred to me! I went home that night and immediately started drawing designs. After the first few, I knew I had discovered what my next book should be about. I am pleased and excited to present seven new quilts, designed especially for this book.

The design for the first wallhanging, NEW DIRECTIONS — NEW BEGINNINGS, uses patterns from my first book, *Celtic Style Floral Appliqué*, as well as two new patterns for baskets and a new border. This quilt is hand quilted with metallic thread and machine quilted with invisible thread.

The second wallhanging, INTERLACED TRACERY, has all new designs, blocks as well as baskets. Originally, I had planned to use five sample blocks in this wallhanging, but then I realized that if I did this, I would have to make more samples! Layout diagrams for both the original version and the finished wallhanging are included. The color choices for this wallhanging were influenced by the currently popular "watercolor" technique (see Bibliography).

For WHOLE CLOTH BASKETS, I asked a friend, Betty McFadyen, to use a new wallhanging design just as a quilting pattern. She hand quilted the design in iridescent metallic thread and I machine quilted the background in a meander pattern with matching thread. I had intended to appliqué the same wallhanging design to show how different it would look, but this idea didn't work out quite as I planned — these things can develop a life of their own! The story of the NIGHTMARE MEDALLION, and how it became two separate wallhangings, INDIAN SUMMER — CHANGES and OUT OF DARKNESS — HOPE, is included in Chapter 3.

SCARLETT'S ROSES was made by another friend, Lois Love, who used one of my patterns in a wallhanging she designed. She has her own unique style and I am glad that she was willing to make a sample to show how my designs could be used with other appliqué patterns. She used one of Elly Sienkiewicz's patterns from her series of books on Baltimore Album quilts (see Bibliography). Lois chose her own colors and hand appliquéd the top. I machine quilted it with invisible thread around all the appliqués and used gold metallic thread for the hand quilting.

The last wallhanging included, FLOWERING BASKETS, is the result of a challenge sponsored by the Quilter's Sew-ciety of Redding. I purchased a packet of fabric and was allowed to add a couple other fabrics to design a small wallhanging. Needless to say, my finished product didn't even look like it used the same fabrics as everyone else's!

I tend to go off in a very different direction when presented with restrictions. Since this has happened to me before, I no longer consider it a fault, but instead indulge it. My friends are used to me doing "really weird" things with shared projects.

My designs are influenced by all the quilts I see and books I read, as well as by any other artwork that I happen across. This inspires endless possibilities for adaptation. I can't imagine running out of ideas. I have a list of what I might want to try next that is growing longer all the time. All the quilt instructions include some of my ideas for variations for each quilt, plus more, in Chapter 4.

You can choose to make a quilt just like one in this book, or you can use the patterns and techniques to come up with your own unique designs. I have been thrilled to receive photos of quilts readers have made from my first book, *Celtic Style Floral Appliqué*. Please send photos of any quilts you make using my designs or for class or lecture information write to: Scarlett Rose, P. O. Box 212, Anderson, CA 96007. I would ask that you give me credit if you enter your quilt in any competitions or if a picture of it is published in a magazine or book. Please contact my publisher if you want to sell the pattern for your quilt to a magazine or book since using my designs in your own quilt would involve the copyright that I hold on all my designs.

Fig. 1-1. *Scarlett Rose's first book, Celtic Style Floral Appliqué.*

Review of Basics

The sewing equipment that you will need to make the quilts in this book are:

  ¼" (6mm) bias bar

  Topstitching or edgestitching foot for your
    sewing machine (optional)

  Hand appliqué needles (Sharps)

  Needle threader (optional)

  Thimble

  Freezer paper (for appliquéing flowers)

  Tracing paper (transparent paper used for
    placing appliqués)

  Rotary cutter, ruler, and mat

  Marking pen or pencil for fabric

  Sewing machine in good working order with
    a new size 12/80 needle

  Paper scissors

  Fabric scissors

  Pins

  Iron (travel size preferred)

  Lamp for hand sewing (optional)

See the Sources section at the end of this book if some items are not available in your area.

In this chapter I explain my method of doing Celtic style appliqué. Please refer to my first book, *Celtic Style Floral Appliqué*, if you need more detailed instructions.

For each quilt in this book, a list of all the sections, blocks and baskets needed is shown in the layout diagram. A couple of the block designs are from my first book, *Celtic Style Floral Appliqué*. However, other blocks in this book may be substi-

tuted. All of the basket designs will work with blocks from the first book. Check the basket patterns for compatible block numbers. The chapter on variations has suggestions for more possible designs.

Measurements are given in each piecing diagram to help you draw a full size pattern of the quilt. When practical, the layout and piecing diagrams are combined into a single diagram. Most of the designs are based on a 6" (15.2cm) grid, so the patterns can be placed together like a puzzle. For example, each complete basket is made up of four 6" (15.2cm) square patterns. The lower two are the basket itself and the upper two block sections form the handle of the basket (see Fig. 2-1). Trace the appropriate patterns from the pattern section onto a single large piece of paper or tape copies togeth-

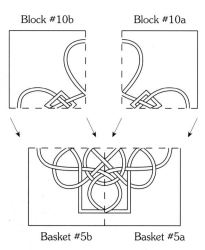

Block #10b   Block #10a

Basket #5b   Basket #5a

Fig. 2-1. *How basket blocks are put together — two basket sections and two block sections.*

er to make a whole design. I draw all my designs this way so I can see what the overall impression will be. Smaller scale drawings don't always show well what the design will look like sewn up in a larger size.

Then trace the complete design onto the background fabric with a fabric marking pen or pencil. The larger quilts are constructed of several background pieces. If the background fabric needs to be pieced together, appliqué as much as possible on each separate background piece before sewing them together.

All the sewn bias strips in this book are ¼" (6mm) wide, made from strips of bias fabric cut ⅞" (23mm) wide. These don't need to be seamed together into one long strip — the ends will be hidden so you often can use short strips. The only time you need to be careful about the length is when the design has strips that run for a distance before the next knot or intersection occurs (see Fig. 2-2). Use the longest strips that you have for those places and the shorter strips for the baskets or blocks.

To prepare a bias strip, fold the strip in half

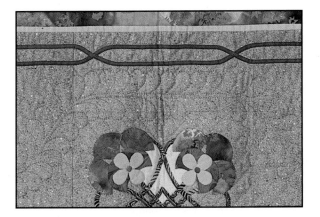

Fig. 2-2. *Close-up of border of New Directions — New Beginnings, showing long bias strips.*

with the right sides out and sew a slightly larger than ¼" (6mm) seam, using the fold as your guide. If you have an edgestitching or topstitching foot for your sewing machine, use it to help you to sew a straight seam. Adjust the guide on the foot so that you are sewing the correct seam width.

Then press the finished strip with the bias bar inside, rolling the seam to one side, so that it will be hidden when the strip is sewn on the background fabric. If you have used tricot lamé or another specialty fabric for the bias strip, use a press cloth and a setting on your iron one lower than cotton when pressing the strip. It is a little more tricky to do this, but the effort is well worth your time. Lamé can really add some sparkle to your quilt.

Insets are pieces of another fabric placed in areas where they are completely surrounded by bias strips. They add interest to the Celtic design by providing contrast, showing off the interlacing. Baste any insets down first, and then begin appliquéing the bias strips. Make sure that the strips cover all the raw edges of the insets. That is what holds them in place. Make sure to leave openings where a strip will be passing underneath the strip you are sewing These intersections are what create the interlaced design. It may take some practice to get into the habit of leaving openings where they are needed. Every other intersection should be open. As you are sewing, double check the pattern to guide you. Some of the more complicated baskets can be very tricky and close attention needs to be paid to make sure the design is done correctly (see Figs. 2-3 through 2-6, page 12).

After all the bias strips are sewn on, appliqué the flowers, if there are any. I use the freezer paper method in which each piece has the seam allowance folded over and pressed to the shiny side of the freezer paper template. That way I can appliqué the pieces down without having to deal with turning under seam allowances as I sew. Use a tracing paper copy of the complete flower as a guideline for placement of the appliqué pieces. Line up the bias strip lines drawn on the tracing paper with the strips you've already appliquéd so you can see where the pieces of the flower need to be placed and appliquéd.

For quilts with several background pieces, when you have completed all the appliqué on the separate pieces, sew the top together and finish any appliqué that crosses over the seams.

I use very thin batting in my quilts. I don't want a very puffy quilt and thicker batting is a lot harder to hand or machine quilt. My preferred batting is Thermore® by Hobbs, a very thin polyester batt. I have also used cotton or cotton blend batting in some of my quilts. Most of my wallhangings are quilted both by hand and machine. I do all the outlining of the bias strips and flowers by machine,

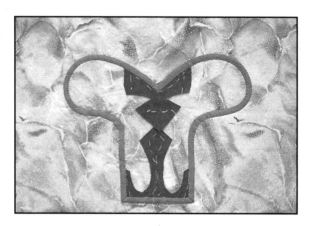

Fig. 2-3. *Insets basted, first strip appliquéd.*

Fig. 2-4. *Adding more strips, interlacing as needed.*

Fig. 2-5. *Last strip in process of being sewn down.*

Fig. 2-6. *Finished block.*

usually with invisible thread. The invisible thread I use is the very fine, very soft kind that resembles a human hair (see Fig. 2-7). The quilting in the open areas of the background fabric is usually done by hand, particularly if there is a design such as a feather.

I started doing a lot of quilting with metallic thread because I think it really adds something to my designs. These threads are a bit more trouble to stitch with than regular thread, but I have discovered a few hints to help keep the problems to a minimum. Look at the metallic thread closely before you buy it. The tighter the twist, the easier it will be to quilt. There are also iridescent threads that are like a thin strip of plastic. These hand quilt beautifully, giving you the shimmering effect of a metallic thread (see Fig. 2-8 and the Sources section at the end of the book). If you are using metallic thread, cut shorter lengths than normal since the thread tends to fray more easily. I use a needle threader for the ones that are not twisted very tightly since they begin to unwind as soon as they are cut. Then, as soon as I pull the needle out of the fabric, I pull on the thread itself rather than the nee-

dle to reduce the wear and tear on the thread where it passes through the eye of the needle. Pull gently and steadily, until the stitches are snug. If you are machine quilting with metallic thread, I have found that the Schmetz Metallica® needle works well. I also sew a little slower than normal and check my tension, too. The Sulky metallic threads sew up beautifully. Since I really like how metallic thread looks quilted in a wallhanging, I am willing to take the extra care required to use it. This is my personal choice. However, please feel free to quilt with regular quilting thread if you prefer. These wallhangings look great quilted with contrasting color thread.

After you are finished quilting, lay the wallhanging flat. Using a long ruler, mark the edges of the quilt so that they are straight and the corners are square (see Fig. 2-9, page 14). Check to see if the quilt sides are the same length side to side and top to bottom. This will help the quilt to hang flat. Trim if necessary. Measure the four sides of this outside edge. Piece together enough bias strips of the binding fabric to equal this measurement plus a little extra for the corners. I cut my strips wide

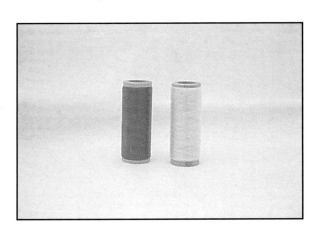

Fig. 2-7. *Dark and clear invisible thread.*

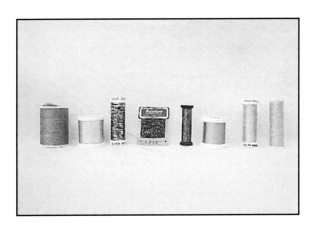

Fig. 2-8. *Different brands and types of metallic thread.*

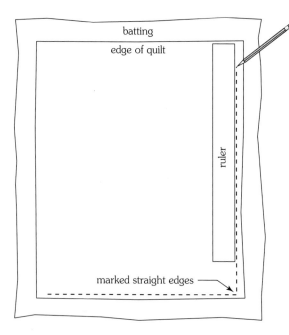

batting

edge of quilt

ruler

marked straight edges

Fig. 2-9. *How to mark edges of quilt for binding.*

enough to make double bias bindings. Press the binding in half lengthwise and sew it to the edge of the wallhanging, following the marked line. Miter the corners and sew the ends together in a miter so it isn't obvious where the binding started. Trim the backing and batting to an even amount, slightly less than the finished width of the binding. Turn the binding to the back of the quilt and sew it down.

Make a hanging sleeve for the finished wall-hanging or quilt, using the same fabric as the back. This can be left on permanently to hang the piece for display. Also sew a label on the back. If the backing is light enough, you can write directly on the fabric using an indelible pen. Be sure to put the date the quilt was finished, the names of everyone who worked on it, and where it was made. If it is a present for someone, include his or her name also.

The Quilts

This book has patterns for seven blocks, eight flower designs, 12 baskets, and 31 sections for borders. These designs can be interchanged with nine blocks and 21 border sections in my first book, *Celtic Style Floral Appliqué*, published by AQS in 1995. References to patterns from this first book are marked (CSFA).

Quilts included in this chapter are:

NEW DIRECTIONS — NEW BEGINNINGS
INTERLACED TRACERY
WHOLE CLOTH BASKETS
NIGHTMARE MEDALLION
INDIAN SUMMER — CHANGES
OUT OF DARKNESS — HOPE
SCARLETT'S ROSES
FLOWERING BASKET

NEW DIRECTIONS — NEW BEGINNINGS

Fig. 3-1. *NEW DIRECTIONS – NEW BEGINNINGS. 64" x 44" (approx. 162.6cm x 111.8cm).*

Fig. 3-2a. *NEW DIRECTIONS — NEW BEGINNINGS. 64" x 44" (162.6cm x 111.8cm).*

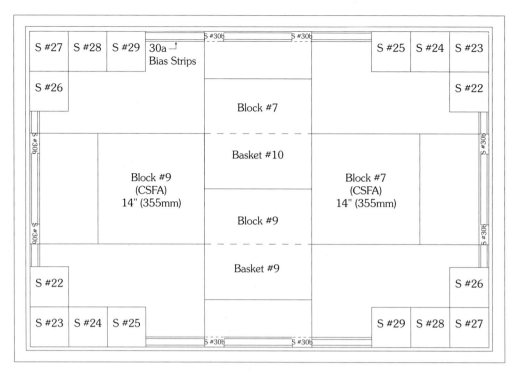

Fig. 3-2b. *NEW DIRECTIONS — NEW BEGINNINGS Layout Diagram.*

Sections #22 – 30 placed 1" (25.4mm) from inside border.

Basket #9 – 14" sq. (356mm)

Basket #10 – 14" sq. (356mm)

Block #7 – 14" sq. (356mm) from CSFA, substitute Block #12 with Flower #14

Block #9 – 14" sq. (356mm) from CSFA, substitute Block #15 with Flower #15a

½" (12.7mm) inside border

1½" (37mm) outside border. Cut 3" (76mm) use 1¾" (44mm) for front, fold 1¼" (32mm) to back.

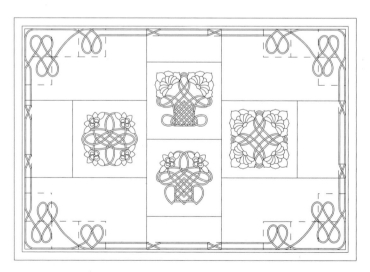

Fig. 3-3. *NEW DIRECTIONS — NEW BEGINNINGS Variation. 62½" x 43" (1089mm x 1583mm). Change Block Block #7 (CSFA) to Block #12 with Flower #14, and change Block #9 (CSFA) to Block #15 with Flower #15a.*

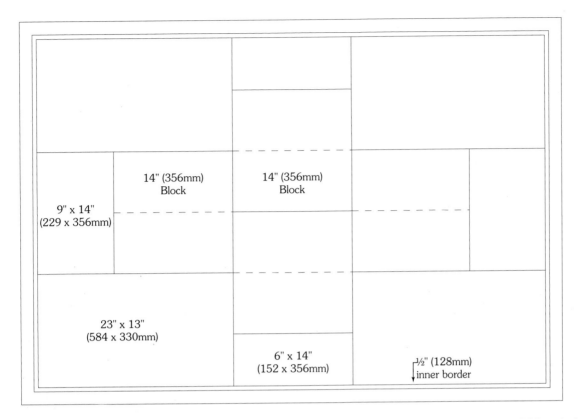

Fig. 3-4. *NEW DIRECTIONS — NEW BEGINNINGS Piecing Diagram. 62½" x 43" (1089mm x 1583mm). Add seam allowances of ¼" (64mm).*

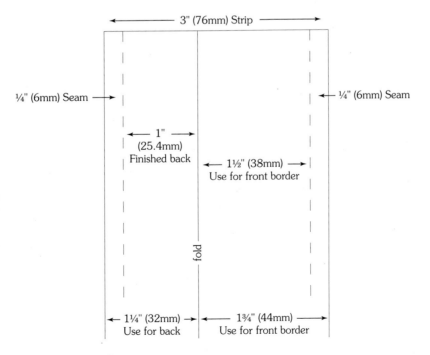

Fig. 3-5. *Border and finished edge diagram.*

INTERLACED TRACERY

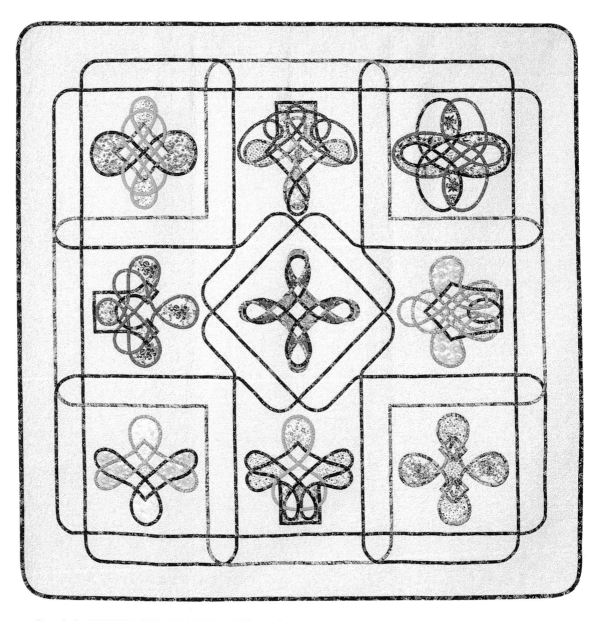

Fig. 3-6. *INTERLACED TRACERY. 53" x 53" (134.3cm x 134.3cm).*

INTERLACED TRACERY

Finished size 53" (134.3cm) square
See Fig. 3-6.

MATERIALS NEEDED:

Fabric (44" or 1.14cm wide):

2½ yds. (2.28m) of printed muslin for background

3 yds. (2.75m) for backing and sleeve

¾ yd. (68.4cm) of dark green print for bias strips and binding

½ yd. (45.7cm) of light green print for bias strips

½ yd. (22.8cm) of the following:

pink print for bias strips and insets

blue print for bias strips and insets

yellow print for bias strips and insets

⅛ yd. (11.4cm) or scraps of 10 different light prints for insets

Matching thread for appliqués

Cream thread for machine quilting

Thin batting

PATTERNS NEEDED:

Sections #31 – 33

Baskets #2, 3, 5 and 6

Blocks #10 – 13 and 15

INSTRUCTIONS:

Draw a full size pattern using the layout diagram for placement of the design elements (see Fig. 3-7b).

The piecing diagram shows how to assemble the top (see Fig. 3-8, page 26). Appliqué as much as possible on the separate pieces, then sew the pieces together and finish appliquéing.

QUILTING:

Quilt by machine using the cream thread, outlining all appliqués and filling in the rest with an overall meandering pattern.

BINDING:

Bind off and attach a sleeve to the back. Don't forget to label the quilt!

VARIATIONS:

• Use different blocks, such as the original designs I had planned to use from *Celtic Style Floral Appliqué* (see Fig. 3-9, page 27).

• Change the corner design using lattice Corner #10 from *Celtic Style Floral Appliqué* (see Fig. 3-10, page 27). Use blocks and baskets from this book.

• Using sections from OUT OF DARKNESS, create a new border. Changes in the lattice will open up the center design. (See Fig. 3-11a, page 28.)

• The last variation shows how I combined INTERLACED TRACERY and NEW DIRECTIONS — NEW BEGINNINGS (Fig. 3-12a, page 30).

Fig. 3-7a. *INTERLACED TRACERY. 53" x 53" (134.3cm x 134.3cm).*

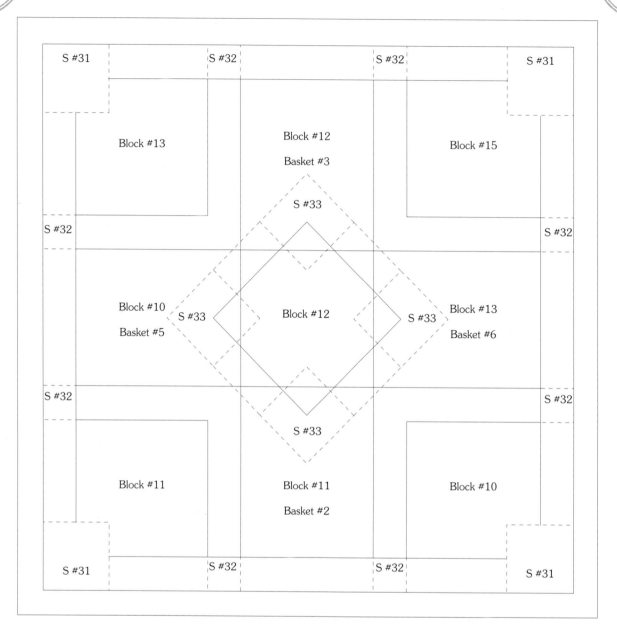

Fig. 3-7b. *INTERLACED TRACERY Layout Diagram.*
Section #31 – 3" (76mm) Lattice corner
Section #32 – 3" (76mm) Lattice edge
Section #33 – 2¾" (??mm) Lattice center block corner
Blocks #10, 11, 12, 13, 15 – 12" sq. (305mm). Rotate design to make complete block pattern in squares marked with block numbers only.

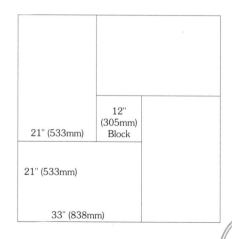

Fig. 3-8 (right). *INTERLACED TRACERY Piecing Diagram. Add seam allowances of ¼" (64mm).*

Fig. 3-9. *INTERLACED TRACERY Variation. 53″ x 53″ (134.3cm x 134.3cm). This variation of INTERLACED TRACERY uses the same layout as Fig. 3-7b with the following changes:*

Block #1 (CSFA) – for Block #13

Block #2 (CSFA) – for Block #10

Block #3 (CSFA) – for Block #11

Block #4 (CSFA) – for Block #15

Block #5 (CSFA) – for Block #12

Fig. 3-10. *INTERLACED TRACERY Variation. 53″ x 53″ (134.3cm x 134.3cm). This variation of INTERLACED TRACERY uses the same layout as Fig. 3-7b, substituting Corner #31 with Corner #10 (CSFA) – Lattice Corner; when using this corner, reverse the intersections of the lattice. Flowers #10 – 17 were added to the blocks.*

Fig. 3-11a. *INTERLACED TRACERY Variation.*

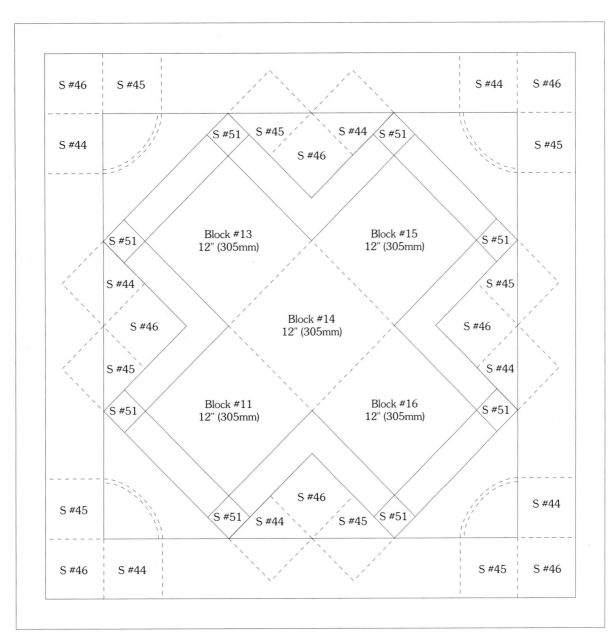

Fig. 3-11b. *INTERLACED TRACERY Variation Layout Diagram.*
Blocks #11, 13, 14, 15, 16
Section #44
Section #45
Section #46
Section #51

Fig. 3-12a. *INTERLACED TRACERY Variation.*

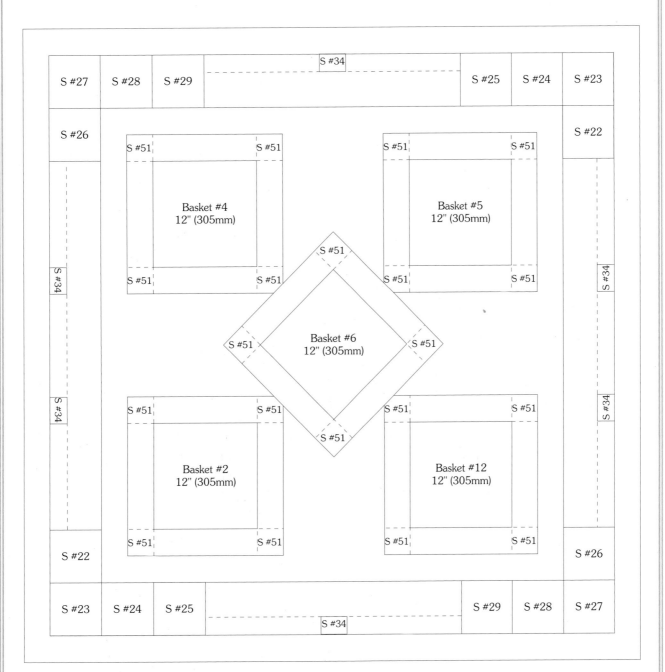

Fig. 3-12b. *INTERLACED TRACERY Variation Layout Diagram.*

Baskets #2, 4, 5, 6, 12

Section #22 – 30

Section #34

Section #51

WHOLE CLOTH BASKETS

Fig. 3-13. *WHOLE CLOTH BASKETS. 60" x 60" (1524mm x 1524mm).*

WHOLE CLOTH BASKETS

Finished size 60" (152.4cm) square
See Fig. 3-13.

This quilt is different from the others in this book in that there is no appliqué. The interlaced designs are quilted into the background fabric.

MATERIALS NEEDED:
    Fabric (44" or 1.14m wide):
        1⅛ yds. (102.9cm) of solid pink for center
        3½ yds. (3.2m) of solid green for border
        4 yds. (3.66m) for backing, sleeve and binding
    Dark iridescent metallic thread
    Pink thread
    Green thread
    Thin batting

PATTERNS NEEDED:
    Sections #35 – 47
    Baskets #7 – 10
    Blocks #6, 6 variation, 7 and 9 from CSFA or substitute Blocks #12 and 13.
    Flowers #15b and 15c

VARIATIONS:
    Use the same layout as Fig. 3-14 making the following changes:
        Block #12 – for Block #7 and 9 (CSFA)
        Block #13 – for Block #6 and 6v (CSFA)

INSTRUCTIONS:

Using the layout diagram, draw a full size copy of the wallhanging (see Fig. 3-14b). Trace the patterns onto the background fabrics. Piece the border onto the center, mitering the corners.

QUILTING:

Hand quilt the design using dark iridescent thread. Machine quilt the center and border in a meandering pattern using matching thread.

BINDING:

Bind off and sew a hanging sleeve on the back. Attach a label or write on the backing with an indelible pen.

VARIATIONS:

- Use several different colors of metallic thread since each basket is made up of at least two separate continuous strips.
- Add flowers to the four baskets in the center.
- Appliqué all the flowers.
- Appliqué the whole design with different colors of bias strips and insets.

Fig. 3-14a. *WHOLE CLOTH BASKETS. 60" x 60" (1524mm x 1524mm).*

S #42	S #41	Basket #7		S #38	S #37	Basket #9		S #40	S #42
S #40	S #39	S #36	S #35	S #36	S #35	S #36	S #35	S #39	S #41
Basket #10	S #35	S #46	S #45	Basket #8		S #44	S #46	S #36	Basket #8
	S #36	S #44	S #43	Block #9 CSFA		S #43	S #45	S #35	
			S #47		S #47				
S #37	S #35	Basket #7	Block #6 CSFA / S #47	S #43	S #43	S #47 / Block #6 CSFA	Basket #9	S #36	S #38
S #38	S #36			S #43	S #43			S #35	S #37
		S #47				S #47			
				S #47	S #47				
Basket #8	S #35	S #45	S #43	Block #7 CSFA		S #43	S #44	S #36	Basket #10
	S #36	S #46	S #44	Basket #10		S #45	S #46	S #35	
S #41	S #39	S #35	S #36	S #35	S #36	S #35	S #36	S #39	S #40
S #42	S #40	Basket #9		S #37	S #38	Basket #7		S #41	S #42

Fig. 3-14b. *WHOLE CLOTH BASKETS Layout Diagram.*

    Sections #35 – 47

    Baskets #7, 8, 9, 10

    Blocks #6, 7, 9, from (CSFA) or substitute Blocks #12, 13

    Flowers #15b, 15c

    Center is 36" (914mm) plus seam allowance

    Border is 12" (305mm)

    Corners are mitered

NIGHTMARE MEDALLION

This quilt was supposed to be an exact copy of WHOLE CLOTH BASKETS. As I started working on it, I made so many mistakes that the name NIGHTMARE MEDALLION became very appropriate. It wasn't until I was three-fourths done with appliquéing the center design that I remembered that I had intended to use more basket designs than just the four in WHOLE CLOTH BASKETS. Some of the new baskets I had designed wouldn't interlace properly into the border lattice so they were to be placed in the center instead. I had figured this out beforehand and wrote all the changes on a piece of paper, but I overlooked this when I began working on the wallhanging. I was then forced to adapt several of the baskets in order to make them fit in the border. I wasn't about to take out all the work I had already done on the center!

I made many other simple mistakes as well. I sewed a strip in the wrong place, not discovering this until after several hours of work had been done! The wrong spots were left open for interweaving. I had trouble sewing some strips correctly along the marked lines. Even when I thought I had fixed all my mistakes, I found a few more as I was quilting the top. I had left a paper template in one leaf and in one spot I hadn't been careful about covering the raw edge of a petal with its neighbor. Both of these mistakes had to be corrected after the top was mostly quilted.

When I had appliquéd three sides of the border, I laid them out on the floor with the center to see how the top looked. It was awful! I hated it and said to myself, "How could I have done such a bad job?!" It has been a long time since any project gave me such a headache! After looking this mess over and over during the next several days, it

became obvious that the only thing to do was to split the original design into two separate wallhangings. The center was fine, but it needed a different border. The original border was wonderful, but really needed a different center design. Twice as much work! But once I decided on this solution, the two wallhangings turned out beautifully.

I complained to my friends about all this, and one friend pointed out that during the time I had been working on this project, I had been under major stress. I had been dealing with grief over losing my last living grandparent, and a few weeks later I suffered a broken heart. This stress apparently affected me so much that I unconsciously worked it into my project. I have purposely worked meanings into other quilts and wallhangings, but this was the first time that I did so without thinking about it.

This revelation about my work was reinforced at a large quilt conference I attended some weeks later. I had volunteered to be a judge's assistant, a very enlightening job for me since I learned how judges come to an agreement on which quilts would receive ribbons. I also listened to all their comments about the quilts. I thought about the reactions I had when I saw particular quilts and found that some created the same response in other viewers. Very effective designing!

I am giving you the original layout diagram (see Fig. 3-15a, page 39) for the NIGHTMARE MEDALLION so that if you like it, you can make this design. The fabric requirements are about the same as for OUT OF DARKNESS — HOPE. I still like this original design, and believe my main problem was with my color choices. Please feel free to make your own choices rather than letting my colors influence you.

NIGHTMARE MEDALLION

Finished size 59" (149.9cm) square
See Fig. 3-15a.

MATERIALS NEEDED:

    Use the amounts of fabric for OUT OF DARKNESS — HOPE, page 50, in your own color choices.

PATTERNS NEEDED:

    Sections #35 – 46
    Baskets #1, 2, 3, 4, 5m, 6m, 7, 8, 9, 10, 11, 12
    Blocks #6, 6 variation, 7, and 9 from (CSFA) or substitute Block #13.
    Flower #15b

VARIATIONS:

- Rearrange the center by dropping the groups of Sections #43, 44, 45 and 46. Overlap Section #46 on each outside corner of the group of Section #43's in the center, leaving the rest of the area blank (Fig. 3-16, page 41).
- Add another border using more of the same sections as the first to make a larger quilt. (Fig. 3-17, page 41).
- Another design could have three baskets in each side of the outer border by leaving out Sections #37 and 38 and placing basket patterns in their place in the center of the outer border.
- Use Flowers #15b and 15c for the center of the design like WHOLE CLOTH BASKETS (Fig. 3-14a, page 35).
- For a different outer border, use Sections #37-38 for the sides, with or without a top loop added, leaving out baskets entirely.
- Add Flower #11 or 12 to Block #13 or to the original blocks from *Celtic Style Floral Appliqué*.

All this redesigning led to the next two finished wallhangings, INDIAN SUMMER — CHANGES and OUT OF DARKNESS — HOPE.

Fig. 3-15a. *NIGHTMARE MEDALLION. 59" x 59" (1499mm x 1499mm).*

S #42	S #41	Basket #5m		S #38	S #37	Basket #12		S #40	S #42
S #40	S #39	S #36	S #35	S #36	S #35	S #36	S #35	S #39	S #41
Basket #11	S #35	S #46	S #45	Basket #9		S #44	S #46	S #36	Basket #2
Basket #11	S #36	S #44	S #43	Block #6 CSFA		S #43	S #45	S #35	Basket #2
S #37	S #35	Basket #8	Block #9 CSFA	S #43	S #43	Block #7 CSFA	Basket #10	S #36	S #38
S #38	S #36	Basket #8	Block #9 CSFA	S #43	S #43	Block #7 CSFA	Basket #10	S #35	S #37
Basket #6m	S #35	S #45	S #43	Block #6 CSFA		S #43	S #44	S #36	Basket #4
Basket #6m	S #36	S #46	S #44	Basket #7		S #45	S #46	S #35	Basket #4
S #41	S #39	S #35	S #36	S #35	S #36	S #35	S #36	S #39	S #40
S #42	S #40	Basket #1		S #37	S #38	Basket #3		S #41	S #42

Fig. 3-15b. *NIGHTMARE MEDALLION Layout Diagram.*

Sections #35 – 46

Baskets #1, 2, 3, 4, 5m, 6m, 7, 8, 9, 10, 11, 12 ("m" indicates baskets needs changes to interlace into border. See basket patterns.)

Blocks #6, 6v, 7, 9 from (CSFA) or substitute Block #13 for all.

Flower #15b

Fig. 3-16. *NIGHTMARE MEDALLION Variation. 59" x 59" (1499mm x 1499mm). This variation of NIGHTMARE MEDALLION uses the same layout as Fig. 3-15b making the following changes:*

Redesign the center by dropping the groups of Sections #43, 44, 45, and 46.

Overlap Section #46 on each outside corner of the group of Section #43's in the center, leaving the rest of the area blank.

Substitute Block #15 for all blocks.

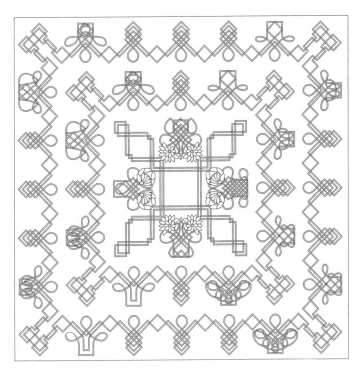

Fig. 3-17. *NIGHTMARE MEDALLION Variation. 84" x 84" (2134mm x 2134mm). This variation of NIGHTMARE MEDALLION uses the same layout as Fig. 3-15b making the following changes:*

Add another border using more of the same sections as the first border to make a larger quilt.

INDIAN SUMMER — CHANGES

Fig. 3-18. *INDIAN SUMMER — CHANGES. 48" x 48" (1219mm x 1219mm).*

INDIAN SUMMER — CHANGES

Finished size: 48" (122 cm) square
See Fig. 3-18.

MATERIALS NEEDED:
  Fabric (44" or 1.14m wide)
    1⅛ yds. (102.9cm) of solid rust for the center
    ⅜ yd. (34.2cm) of black tricot lamé for bias strips
    ½ yd. (45.7cm) of blue tricot lamé for bias strips and flowers
    ⅛ yd. (11.4cm) of yellow print for flower centers
    ¼ yd. (22.8cm) of green print for leaves
    ¼ yd. (22.8cm) of solid black for narrow border and flowers
    1½ yds. (137.2cm) of print for bias strips, binding and wide border
    3 yds. (2.75m) for backing and sleeve
  Dark iridescent metallic thread
  Rust quilting thread
  Brown quilting thread
  Invisible thread
  Thin batting

PATTERNS NEEDED:
  Sections #43– 47
  Baskets #7 – 10
  Blocks #6, 6 variation, 7 and 9 from (CSFA) or substitute Blocks #12 and 13.
  Flower #15b

INSTRUCTIONS:

Using the layout diagram, draw a full size copy of the design (see Fig. 3-19b, page 46). The diagram also shows how the top is put together. Appliqué the center before piecing the top.

QUILTING:

Machine quilt around all the appliqués with invisible thread. Hand quilt the feathers with the dark iridescent metallic thread (I drew the feathers freehand). Use rust quilting thread to quilt diagonal lines in the lattice. Space the lines ½" (13mm) apart. Using the brown quilting thread for the border, quilt diagonal lines ½" (13mm) apart.

BINDING:

Bind the quilt and add a hanging sleeve and label to the back.

VARIATIONS:

- Add the border design using Sections #43 – 47 (see Fig. 3-20b, page 48), moving the baskets to the border and changing the center lattice.
- Use Flower #15c for the center.
- Appliqué the flowers with complete blocks.

Fig. 3-19a. *INDIAN SUMMER — CHANGES. 48" x 48" (1219mm x 1219mm).*

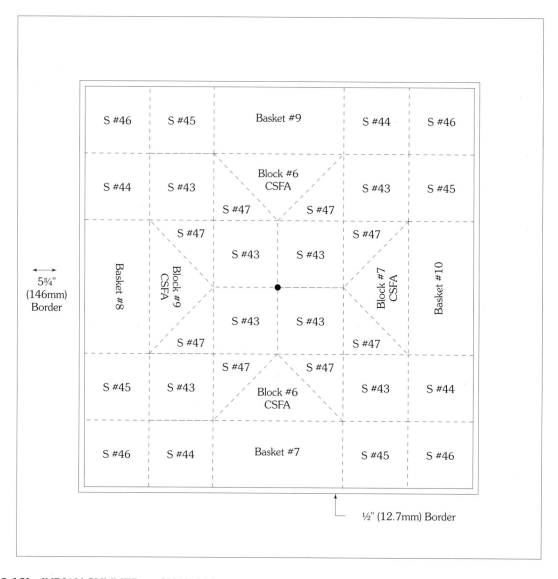

Fig. 3-19b. *INDIAN SUMMER — CHANGES Layout Diagram.*

Sections #43 – 47

Baskets #7, 8, 9, 10

Blocks #6, 6 variation, 7, 9 from CSFA or substitute Block #13 for all.

Flower #15b

Center is 36" (914mm)

Inner border is ½" (12.7mm)

Outer border is 5¾" (146mm) plus seam allowance.

Fig. 3-20a. *INDIAN SUMMER — CHANGES Variation. 60" x 60" (1524mm x 1524mm).*

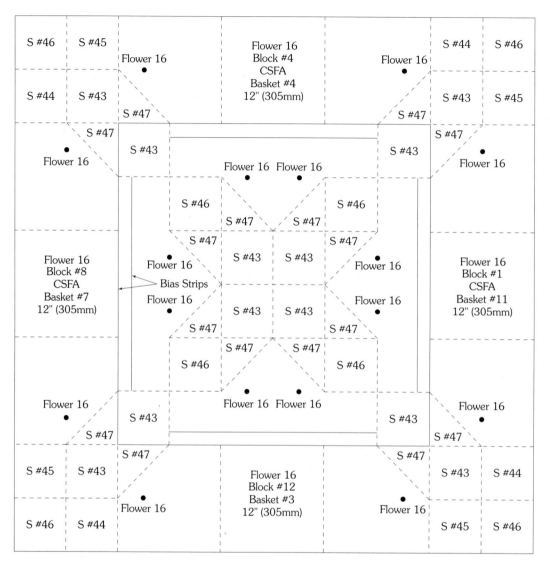

Fig. 3-20b. *INDIAN SUMMER — CHANGES Variation Layout Diagram. 60" x 60" (1524mm x 1524mm).*

Sections #43 – 47

Baskets #4, 7, 11, 13

Blocks #4, 8, 1, 12

Flower #16

• Dot indicates where to place Flower #16, mirror imaging for left and right facing flowers. 6" (152mm) down from center block of Section #43's and 3¼" (82mm) from corner of Section #46 for center. 6" (152mm) from edge of quilt and 3¼" (82mm) from Sections #44 and #45 for border.

OUT OF DARKNESS — HOPE

Fig. 3-21. *OUT OF DARKNESS — HOPE. 59" x 59" (149.9cm x 149.9cm).*

OUT OF DARKNESS — HOPE

Finished size: 59" (149.9cm) square
See Fig. 3-21.

MATERIALS NEEDED:
  Fabric (44" or 1.14m wide):
    1⅛ yd. (102.9cm) of solid black for center
    ¾ yd. (68.4cm) of gold tricot lamé for bias strips
    ¾ yd. (68.4cm) of brown print for bias strips
    ½ yd. (45.7cm) of black tricot lamé for bias strips
    3½ yds. (3.2m) of solid blue for the border
    3½ yds. (3.2m) for backing and sleeve
  Black thread
  Blue thread to match solid blue border
  Gold metallic thread
  Invisible thread
  Thin batting

PATTERNS NEEDED:
  Sections #35 – 42
  Baskets #1 – 4, 5 modified, 6 modified, 9, 11 and 12
  Block #9 from CSFA or substitute Block #13

INSTRUCTIONS:

Using the layout and piecing diagram, draw a full size copy of the design (see Fig. 3-22b, page 53). Cut the background fabrics as shown in Fig. 3-21, page 49. Trace the design onto the background fabrics. You may need a lightbox or window to trace the design on dark fabric. Appliqué the center and each of the four sides. Finish the appliquéing after piecing the top together.

QUILTING:

Machine quilt around all the appliqués with invisible thread. Then hand quilt the feathers with gold metallic thread. Fill in the background with machine quilting done in matching thread.

BINDING:

Bind off and attach the hanging sleeve. Sew on a label or write on the backing with an indelible pen.

VARIATIONS:

- For a different border, use only Sections #35 – 38 so there aren't any baskets, with or without the top loop added (see Fig. 3-23a, page 54).
- This design could also be altered into a rectangle, hanging either vertically or horizontally (see Fig. 3-24a, page 56).
- Add another border using more of the same sections as the first to make a larger rectangular quilt.
- Another variation of Fig. 3-23a could have three baskets on each side of inner border and five baskets in the center.

Fig. 3-22a. *OUT OF DARKNESS — HOPE. 59" x 59" (149.9cm x 149.9cm).*

S #42	S #41	Basket #5m		S #38	S #37	Basket #12		S #40	S #42
S #40	S #39	S #36	S #35	S #36	S #35	S #36	S #35	S #39	S #41
Basket #11	S #35	S #42	S #41	S #38	S #37	S #40	S #42	S #36	Basket #2
	S #36	S #40	S #39	S #36	S #35	S #39	S #41	S #35	
S #37	S #35	S #37	S #35	Block #9 CSFA Basket #9 12" (305mm)		S #36	S #38	S #36	S #38
S #38	S #36	S #38	S #36			S #35	S #37	S #35	S #37
Basket #6m	S #35	S #41	S #39	S #35	S #36	S #39	S #40	S #36	Basket #4
	S #36	S #42	S #40	S #37	S #38	S #41	S #42	S #35	
S #41	S #39	S #35	S #36	S #35	S #36	S #35	S #36	S #39	S #40
S #42	S #40	Basket #1		S #37	S #38	Basket #3		S #41	S #42

Fig. 3-22b. *OUT OF DARKNESS — HOPE Layout Diagram.*

Sections #35 – 42

Baskets #12, 3, 4, 5m, 6m, 9, 11, 12 ("m" indicates these baskets need changes to interlace into border. See basket patterns.)

Block #9 (CSFA) or substitute Block #13

Center is 36" (914mm)

Border is 12" (305mm) plus seam allowance.

Corners are mitered.

Fig. 3-23a. *OUT OF DARKNESS — HOPE Variation. 84" x 84" (2134mm x 2134mm).*

S #42	S #41	S #38	S #37	S #38	S #37	S #38	S #37	S #38	S #37	S #38	S #37	S #40	S #41
Flower 12		*Flower 13*		*Flower 14*		*Flower 14*		*Flower 13*		*Flower 12*			
S #40	S #39	S #36	S #35	S #36	S #35	S #36	S #35	S #36	S #35	S #36	S #35	S #39	S #42
Flower 12 S #37	S #35	S #42	S #41	Basket #5m		S #38	S #37	Basket #12		S #40	S #42	*Flower 12* S #36	S #38
S #38	S #36	S #40	S #39	S #36	S #35	S #36	S #35	S #36	S #35	S #39	S #41	S #35	S #37
Flower 13 S #37	S #35	Basket #11	S #35	S #42	S #41	S #38	S #37	S #40	S #42	S #36	Basket #2	*Flower 13* S #36	S #38
				Flower 11		*Flower 11*							
S #38	S #36		S #36	S #40	S #39	S #36	S #35	S #39	S #42	S #35		S #35	S #37
Flower 14 S #37	S #35	S #37	S #35	*Flower 11* S #37	S #35	Block #14 Basket #5 12" (305mm) Flower 15a		*Flower 11* S #36	S #38	S #36	S #38	*Flower 14* S #36	S #38
S #38	S #36	S #38	S #36	S #38	S #36			S #35	S #37	S #35	S #37	S #35	S #37
Flower 14 S #37	S #35	Basket #6m	S #35	*Flower 11* S #41	S #39	S #35	S #36	*Flower 11* S #39	S #40	S #36	Basket #4	*Flower 14* S #36	S #38
				Flower 11		*Flower 11*							
S #38	S #36		S #36	S #42	S #40	S #37	S #38	S #41	S #42	S #35		S #35	S #37
Flower 13 S #37	S #35	S #41	S #39	S #35	S #36	S #35	S #36	S #35	S #36	S #39	S #40	*Flower 13* S #36	S #38
S #38	S #36	S #42	S #40	Basket #1		S #37	S #38	Basket #3		S #41	S #42	S #35	S #37
Flower 12 S #41	S #39	S #35	S #36	S #35	S #36	S #35	S #36	S #35	S #36	S #35	S #36	*Flower 12* S #39	S #40
		Flower 12		*Flower 13*		*Flower 14*		*Flower 14*		*Flower 13*		*Flower 12*	
S #42	S #40	S #37	S #38	S #37	S #38	S #37	S #38	S #37	S #38	S #37	S #38	S #41	S #42

Fig. 3-23b. *OUT OF DARKNESS — HOPE Variation Layout Diagram. 84" x 84" (2134mm x 2134mm).*

Sections #35 – 42 use variations with top loop and extra square

Basket #5

Block #14

Flowers #11, 12, 13, 14, 15a

Fig. 3-24a. *OUT OF DARKNESS — HOPE Variation. 60" x 36" (152.4cm x 91.4cm). This design variation will also work vertically; use the same border, rotating the basket blocks one-quarter turn counterclockwise.*

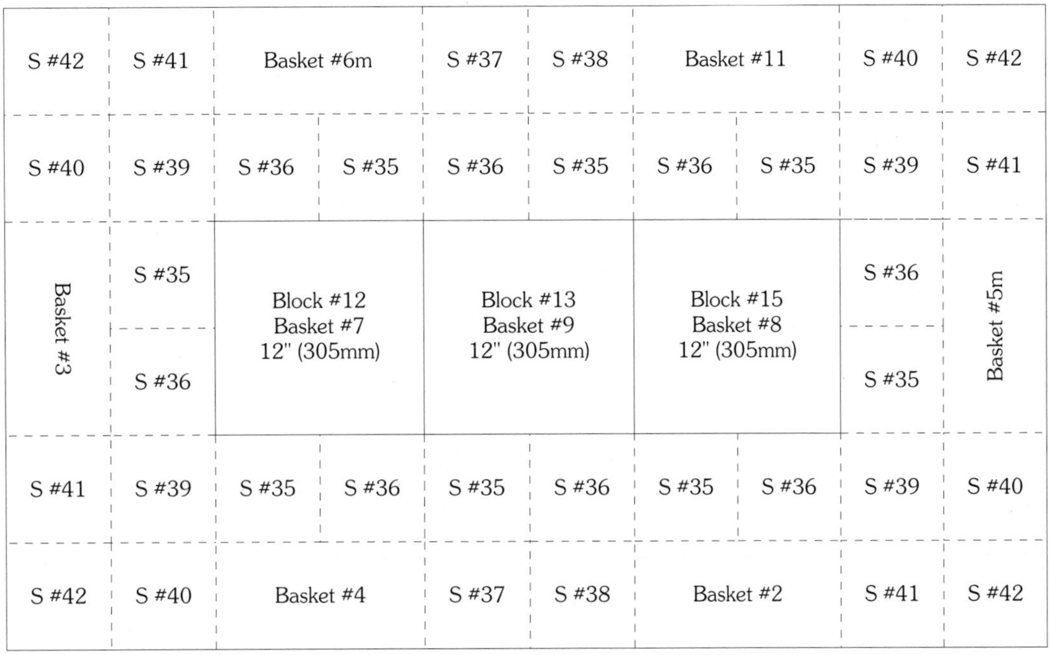

Top diagram:

S #42	S #41	Basket #6m		S #37	S #38	Basket #11		S #40	S #42
S #40	S #39	S #36	S #35	S #36	S #35	S #36	S #35	S #39	S #41
Basket #3	S #35 / S #36	Block #12 Basket #7 12" (305mm)		Block #13 Basket #9 12" (305mm)		Block #15 Basket #8 12" (305mm)		S #36 / S #35	Basket #5m
S #41	S #39	S #35	S #36	S #35	S #36	S #35	S #36	S #39	S #40
S #42	S #40	Basket #4		S #37	S #38	Basket #2		S #41	S #42

Fig. 3-24b. *OUT OF DARKNESS — HOPE Variation Layout Diagrams. 60" x 36" (152.4cm x 91.4cm).*

> Sections #35 – 42
>
> Baskets #2, 3, 4, 5m, 6m, 8, 9, 11 ("m" indicates these baskets need changes to interlace into the border. See basket patterns.)
>
> Blocks #12, 13, 15

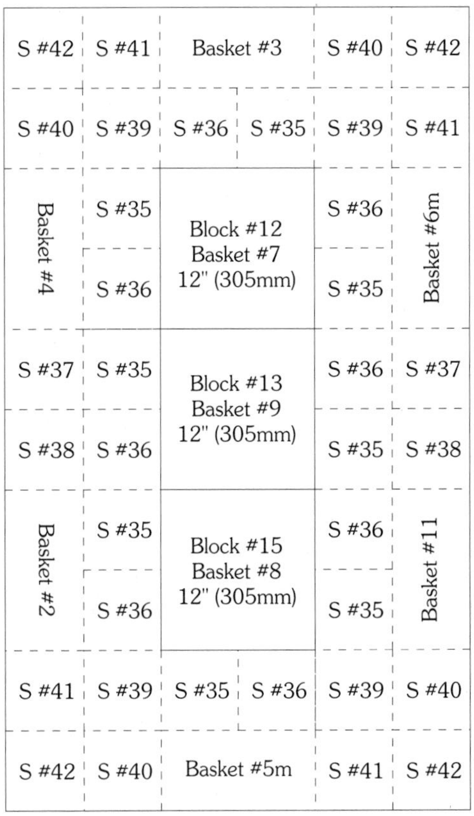

Bottom-right diagram:

S #42	S #41	Basket #3		S #40	S #42
S #40	S #39	S #36	S #35	S #39	S #41
Basket #4	S #35 / S #36	Block #12 Basket #7 12" (305mm)		S #36 / S #35	Basket #6m
S #37 / S #38	S #35 / S #36	Block #13 Basket #9 12" (305mm)		S #36 / S #35	S #37 / S #38
Basket #2	S #35 / S #36	Block #15 Basket #8 12" (305mm)		S #36 / S #35	Basket #11
S #41	S #39	S #35	S #36	S #39	S #40
S #42	S #40	Basket #5m		S #41	S #42

SCARLETT'S ROSES

Fig. 3-25. *SCARLETT'S ROSES. 47" x 47" (1194mm x 1194mm).*

SCARLETT'S ROSES

Finished size 47" (119cm) square
See Fig. 3-25.

MATERIALS NEEDED:
 Fabric (44" or 1.14m wide)
  ⅞ yd. (79.8cm) of solid teal for blocks
  ⅞ yd. (79.8cm) of solid wine for blocks
  1½ yds. (137.2cm) of purple for center block and border
  1½ yds. (137.2cm) of multicolor solid for bias strips and lattice
  2¾ yds. (228.7cm) for backing and sleeve
  ¼ yd. (22.8cm) of green print for flower stems
  assorted scraps of green prints for leaves
  ¾ yd. (68.4cm) of red print for bias strips
  ¼ yd. (22.8cm) of red print for roses and buds
  ⅛ yd. (11.4cm) each of two different pink prints for roses
  ⅛ yd. (11.4cm) of white print for roses
 Gold metallic thread
 Invisible thread
 Thin batting

PATTERNS NEEDED:
 Sections #48 and 49
 Basket #1
 Block #1 (CSFA) or substitute Block #12 or 13
 Section #50 – Celtic Rose Wreath

 The fan block is from *Baltimore Album Quilts* by Elly Sienkiewicz (Pattern #39, "Albertine's Rose Climber," on pages 84-87). Or substitute Section #50 or one of Blocks #10 – 16 with flowers for the corners instead.

INSTRUCTIONS:

Use the layout and piecing diagram as a guide for placement of the blocks (see Fig. 3-26b, page 62). Appliqué each block, then piece the top together and appliqué the border design, using Section #49 for the corner appliqué.

QUILTING:

Machine quilt with invisible thread around all the appliqués and along the lattice. Hand quilt with gold metallic thread ½" (13mm) diagonal lines in the basket blocks, the handle in the fan blocks and use Section #48 three times on each side as a quilting design in the border.

BINDING:

Bind off, attaching a hanging sleeve and label to the back of the quilt.

VARIATIONS:

- Use Blocks #12 – 16 in place of the fans and the wreath center (see Fig. 3-27, page 63).
- Use Baskets #1, 7, 8 and 12 with suitable blocks (see Fig. 3-28, page 63).

Fig. 3-26a. *SCARLETT'S ROSES. 47" x 47" (1194mm x 1194mm).*

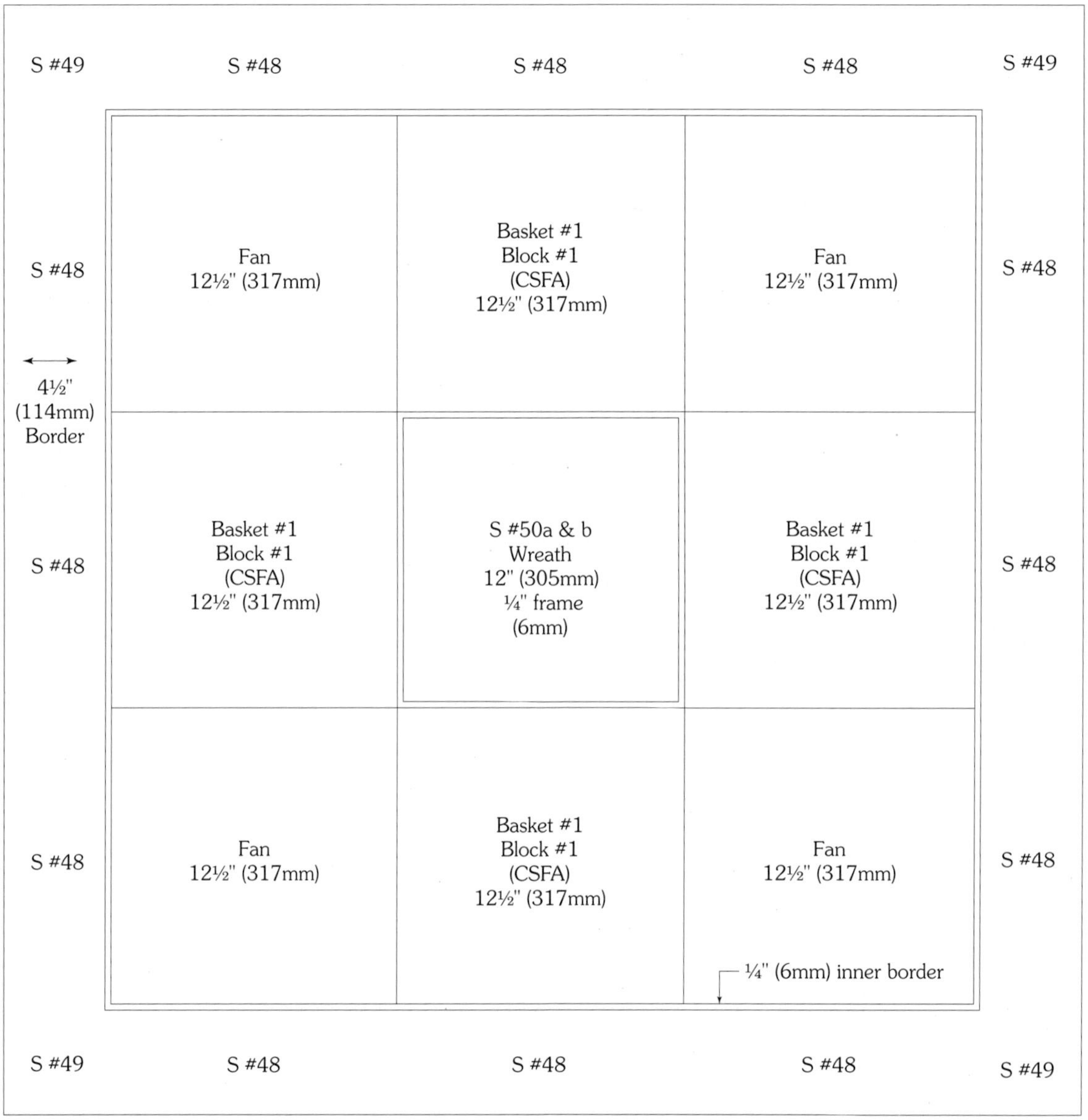

S #49	S #48	S #48	S #48	S #49

| S #48 | Fan
12½" (317mm) | Basket #1
Block #1
(CSFA)
12½" (317mm) | Fan
12½" (317mm) | S #48 |

4½"
(114mm)
Border

| S #48 | Basket #1
Block #1
(CSFA)
12½" (317mm) | S #50a & b
Wreath
12" (305mm)
¼" frame
(6mm) | Basket #1
Block #1
(CSFA)
12½" (317mm) | S #48 |

| S #48 | Fan
12½" (317mm) | Basket #1
Block #1
(CSFA)
12½" (317mm) | Fan
12½" (317mm) | S #48 |

— ¼" (6mm) inner border

| S #49 | S #48 | S #48 | S #48 | S #49 |

Fig. 3-26b. *SCARLETT'S ROSES Layout Diagram.*

Sections #48, 49, 50

Basket #1

Block #1 (CSFA)

Center is 12" (305mm) with ¼" frame.

8 – 12½" (317mm) blocks surround center.

¼" lattice

4½" (114mm) border – bias strip 2¼" (57mm) from inside edge.

Fig. 3-27. *SCARLETT'S ROSES Variation. 47" x 47" (1194mm x 1194mm). This variation of SCARLETT'S ROSES uses the same layout as Fig. 3-26b with the following changes:*

Use block designs in place of the fans and the wreath center.

Blocks # 12, 13, 14, 15, 16

Fig. 3-28. *SCARLETT'S ROSES Variation. 47" x 47" (1194mm x 1194mm). This variation of SCARLETT'S ROSES uses the same layout as Fig. 3-26b with the following changes:*

Use four different baskets instead of just one and baskets instead of fans and wreath.

Basket # 1 – Block #1 (CSFA)   Basket #1 replaces wreath or fans.

Basket # 7 – Block #7 (CSFA)   Basket #4 replaces wreath or fans.

Basket # 8 – Block #8 (CSFA)   Basket #7 replaces wreath or fans.

Basket # 12 – Block #4 (CSFA)   Basket #8 replaces wreath or fans.

Alternately flip Section #48 in border.   Basket #9 replaces wreath or fans.

FLOWERING BASKET

Fig. 3-29. *FLOWERING BASKET. 19½" x 19½" (49.5cm x 49.5cm).*

FLOWERING BASKET

Finished size 19½" (49.5cm) square
See Fig. 3-29.

MATERIALS NEEDED:

Fabric (44" or 1.14m wide):

⅝ yd. (57cm) for backing and sleeve

⅜ yd. (34.2cm) of tan print for block

¼ yd. (22.8cm) of dark green print for leaves, strips and binding

⅛ yd. (11.4cm) of dark green solid for leaves

¼ yd. (22.8cm) of white print for border

¼ yd. (22.8cm) of brown print for bias strips

⅛ yd. (11.4cm) of marbled purple for flowers

6" (152mm) square of yellow print for flowers

2" (50mm) square of orange print for flower centers

Dark iridescent metallic thread

Metallic thread

Thin batting

PATTERNS NEEDED:

Basket #6

Block #6 from (CSFA) with Flower #10 or substitute Block #13 with Flower #11 or 12

INSTRUCTIONS:

Make a full size copy of the center block, transfer it to the background fabric, and appliqué. Piece the top together following the layout diagram (see Fig. 3-30b).

QUILTING:

Hand quilt around all the appliqués with the dark iridescent metallic thread, and then in ⅞" (22mm) diagonal lines across the block with the gold metallic thread. (The diagonal lines in the border slant in the opposite direction from those in the center block.)

BINDING:

Bind off and attach a hanging sleeve and label to the back.

VARIATION:

This small wallhanging would make an attractive pillow, using any of the basket patterns for the center.

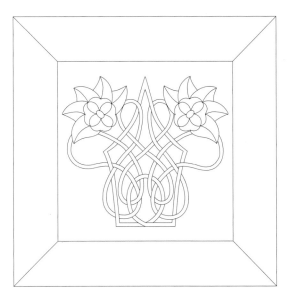

Fig. 3-30a. *FLOWERING BASKETS. 19½" x 19½" (49.5cm x 49.5cm).*

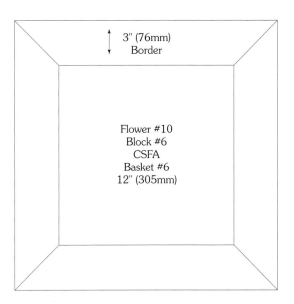

3" (76mm)
Border

Flower #10
Block #6
CSFA
Basket #6
12" (305mm)

Fig. 3-30b. *FLOWERING BASKETS Layout Diagram. 19½" x 19½" (49.5cm x 49.5cm).*

Basket #6

Block #6 (CSFA) with Flower #10 or substitute Block #13 with Flower #11 or #12.

Miter corners of border.

More Variations

As usual, I can think of so many different ways to redo my designs. I have included many of these possible variations in this book since I will probably never have enough time to do them myself. Here are some more ideas:

- Using the lattice and border of CELTIC ORCHIDS from *Celtic Style Floral Appliqué,* (CSFA) substitute the baskets for flower blocks (see Fig. 4-1a).

- Using INTERLACED TRACERY variation in Figs.4-2 and 4-3, pages 71–74, use border designs from CSFA instead of plainer lattice to create a more intricate design.

- Beginning with the INDIAN SUMMER — CHANGES Variation in Fig.3-20a, page 47, substitute a pattern of four basket parts for the patterns made of two block parts and two basket parts and changing the flowers (see Fig. 4-4, page 75).

- Use blocks made of four Basket parts in the layout for INTERLACED DIAMONDS from *Celtic Style Floral Appliqué* (Fig. 4-5a, page 76).

- I redesigned Flower #15, creating two variations, #15b and #15c, to fill in spaces between interlacing. The same could be done with the other flowers from this book as well as those from *Celtic Style Floral Appliqué.* You could also use flowers from other sources or design your own.

- All the blocks, baskets, and variations in this book can be interchanged with the layouts from my first book, so try out different combinations and create your own variation.

Fig. 4-1a. *CELTIC ORCHIDS Variation. 78" X 78" (2m x 2m).*

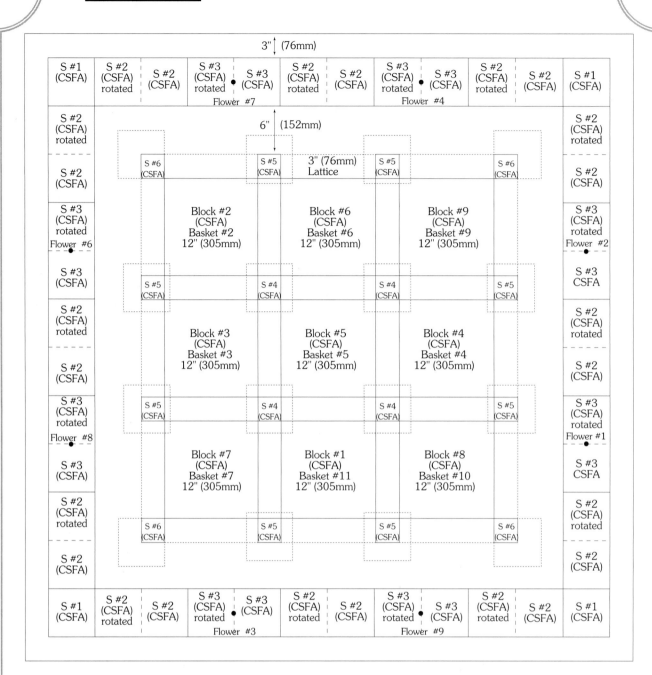

3" (76mm)

| S #1 (CSFA) | S #2 (CSFA) rotated | S #2 (CSFA) | S #3 (CSFA) rotated | S #3 (CSFA) | S #2 (CSFA) rotated | S #2 (CSFA) | S #3 (CSFA) rotated | S #3 (CSFA) | S #2 (CSFA) rotated | S #2 (CSFA) | S #1 (CSFA) |

Flower #7   Flower #4

6" (152mm)

| S #2 (CSFA) rotated | | | | | | | | | | | S #2 (CSFA) rotated |

| S #2 (CSFA) | | S #6 (CSFA) | | S #5 (CSFA) | 3" (76mm) Lattice | S #5 (CSFA) | | S #6 (CSFA) | | | S #2 (CSFA) |

| S #3 (CSFA) rotated | | Block #2 (CSFA) Basket #2 12" (305mm) | | | Block #6 (CSFA) Basket #6 12" (305mm) | | | Block #9 (CSFA) Basket #9 12" (305mm) | | | S #3 (CSFA) rotated |

Flower #6   Flower #2

| S #3 (CSFA) | | S #5 (CSFA) | | S #4 (CSFA) | | S #4 (CSFA) | | S #5 (CSFA) | | | S #3 CSFA |

| S #2 (CSFA) rotated | | Block #3 (CSFA) Basket #3 12" (305mm) | | | Block #5 (CSFA) Basket #5 12" (305mm) | | | Block #4 (CSFA) Basket #4 12" (305mm) | | | S #2 (CSFA) rotated |

| S #2 (CSFA) | | | | | | | | | | | S #2 (CSFA) |

| S #3 (CSFA) rotated | | S #5 (CSFA) | | S #4 (CSFA) | | S #4 (CSFA) | | S #5 (CSFA) | | | S #3 (CSFA) rotated |

Flower #8   Flower #1

| S #3 (CSFA) | | Block #7 (CSFA) Basket #7 12" (305mm) | | | Block #1 (CSFA) Basket #11 12" (305mm) | | | Block #8 (CSFA) Basket #10 12" (305mm) | | | S #3 CSFA |

| S #2 (CSFA) rotated | | | | | | | | | | | S #2 (CSFA) rotated |

| S #2 (CSFA) | | S #6 (CSFA) | | S #5 (CSFA) | | S #5 (CSFA) | | S #6 (CSFA) | | | S #2 (CSFA) |

| S #1 (CSFA) | S #2 (CSFA) rotated | S #2 (CSFA) | S #3 (CSFA) rotated | S #3 (CSFA) | S #2 (CSFA) rotated | S #2 (CSFA) | S #3 (CSFA) rotated | S #3 (CSFA) | S #2 (CSFA) rotated | S #2 (CSFA) | S #1 (CSFA) |

Flower #3   Flower #9

Fig. 4-1b. *CELTIC ORCHIDS Variation Layout Diagram. This variation of CELTIC ORCHIDS uses the same layout as Fig. 6-2a, page 37 (CSFA), making the following changes:*

Block #2 – Basket #2

Block #6 – Basket #6

Block #9 – Basket #9

Block #3 – Basket #3

Block #5 – Basket #5

Block #4 – Basket #4

Block #7 – Basket #7

Block #1 – Basket #11

Block #8 – Basket #10

• Dot indicates where flowers are placed, 2¼" from inside border.

Fig. 4-2a. *INTERLACED TRACERY Variation. 53" x 53" (134.3cm x 134.3cm)*

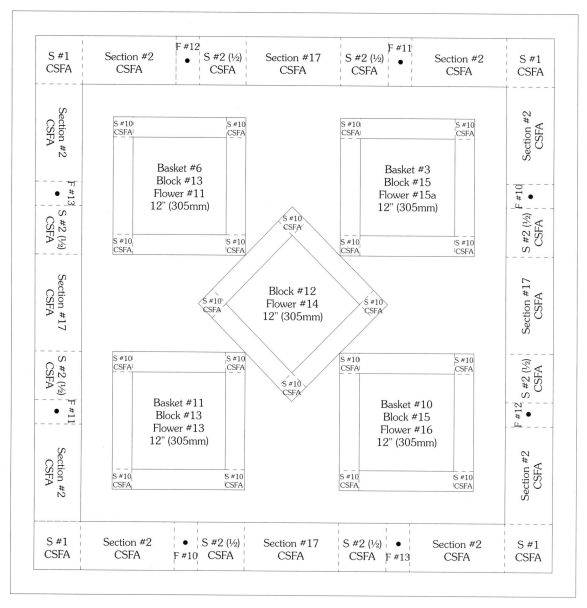

Fig. 4-2b. *INTERLACED TRACERY Variation Layout Diagram.*

Baskets #3, 6, 10, 11 – 12" sq. (305mm)

Blocks #12, 13, 15 – 12" sq. (305mm)

Flowers #10, 11, 12, 13, 14 (all four corners of Block #12), 15a, 16, 15a

Section #1 (CSFA) – Corner unit – 6" sq.

Section #2 (CSFA) – Border knot – 6" x 12"

Section #2 (CSFA) – ½ of Border knot – 6" sq.

Section #10 (CSFA) – Lattice corner – 3" sq.

Section #10m (CSFA) – Lattice corner modified

Section #17 (CSFA) – Fancy knot – 6" x 12" — modify by eliminating strips that deadend.

• Dot indicates where flowers are placed, 2¼" from inside border.

Fig. 4-3a. *INTERLACED TRACERY Variation. 60" x 60" (152.4cm x 152.4cm)*

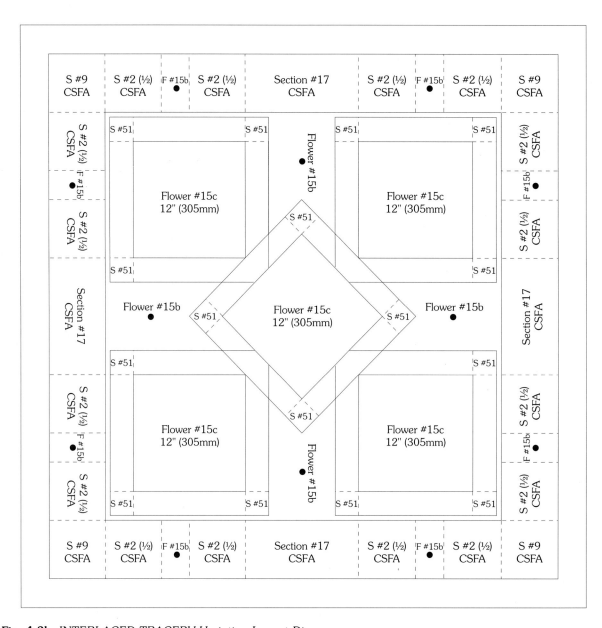

Fig. 4-3b. *INTERLACED TRACERY Variation Layout Diagram.*

Flowers #15b, 15c

Section #51

Section #2 (CSFA) – ½ of Border knot – 6" sq.

Section #9 (CSFA) – Corner unit knot – 6" sq.

Section #17 (CSFA) – Fancy knot – 6" x 12"

• Dot indicates where flowers are placed, 2¼" from inside border.

Fig. 4-4. *INDIAN SUMMER — CHANGES Variation. 60" x 60" (1524mm x 1524mm). This variation of INDIAN SUMMER — CHANGES uses the same layout as Fig. 3-20b, page 48, making the following changes:*

Change basket and blocks to all baskets.

Use a pattern made of 4 basket sections for each design.

Change Flower #16 to Flowers #15a, 15b, and 15c

Fig. 4-5a. *INTERLACED DIAMONDS Variation. 90" x 90" (2286mm x 2286mm).*

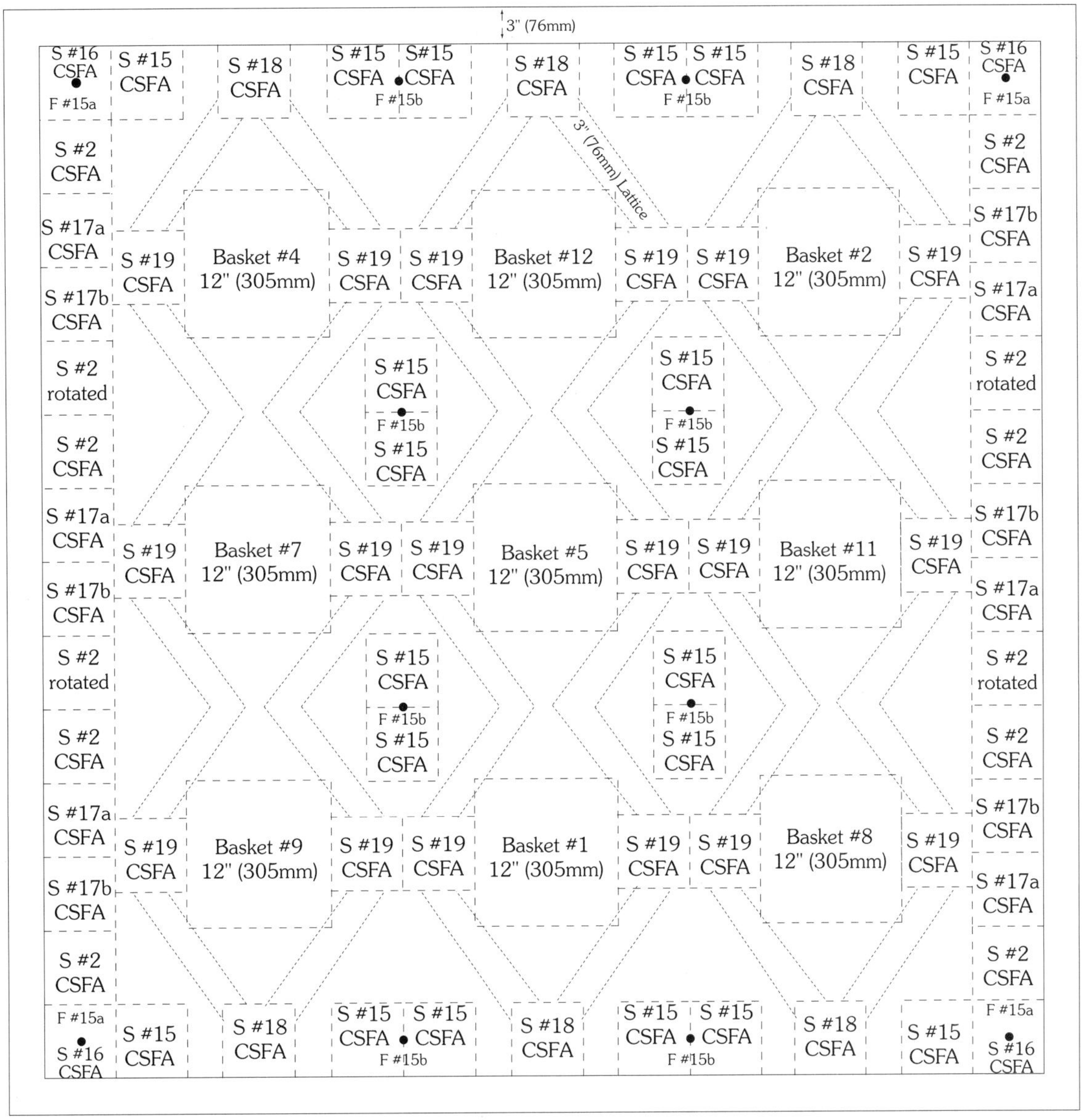

Fig. 4-5b. *INTERLACED DIAMONDS Variation Layout Diagram. 60" x 60" (1524mm x 1524mm). This variation of INTERLACED DIAMONDS uses the same layout as (CSFA) Fig. 7-6a, page 79, making the following changes:*

Replace Block #1 with Baskets #1, 2, 4, 5, 7, 8, 9, 11, and 12 (place as indicated) used in all four sections of 12" squares to form design. Use Flowers 15a, 15b.

• Dot indicates where flowers are placed, 2¼" from inside border.

The Section Patterns

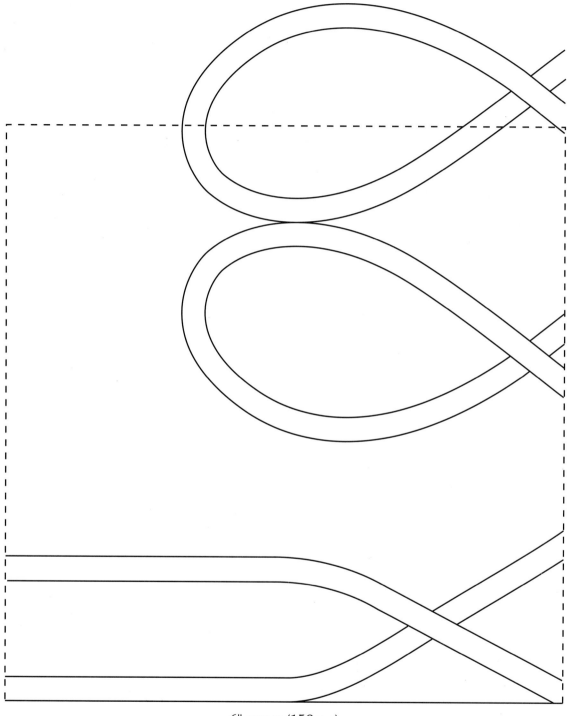

6" square (152mm)

Section #22

Patterns for Border Sections #1 – 21 are given in my first book, *Celtic Style Floral Appliqué*; the border sections in this book begin with #22.

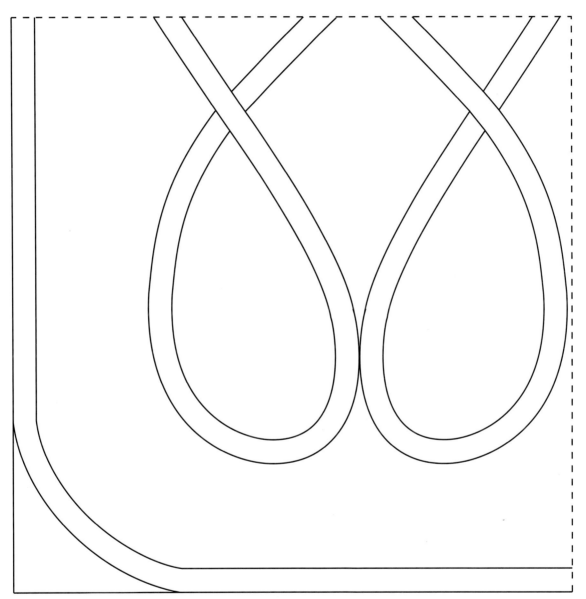

6" square (152mm)

Section #23

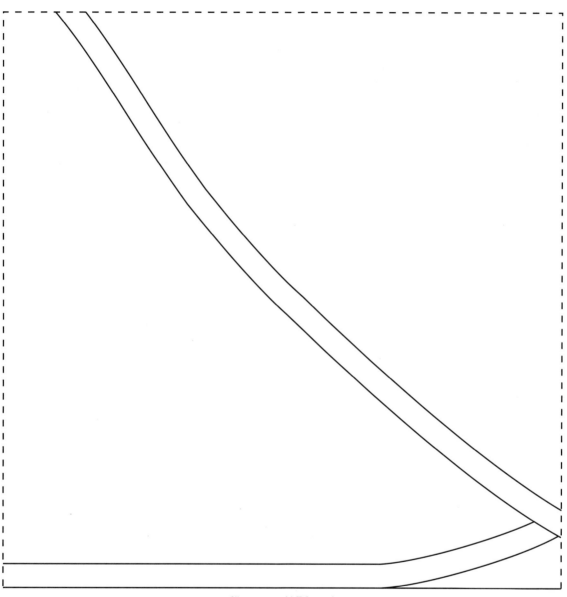

6" square (152mm)

Section #24

6" square (152mm)

Section #25

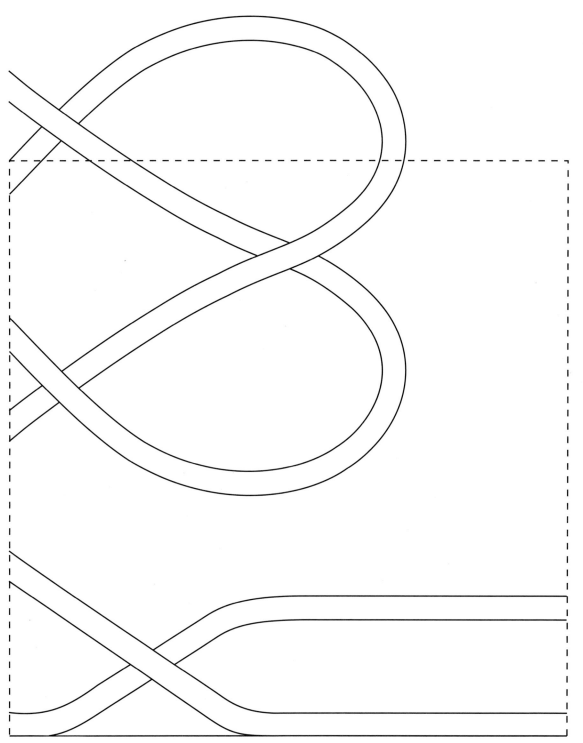

6" square (152mm) within dotted lines

Section #26

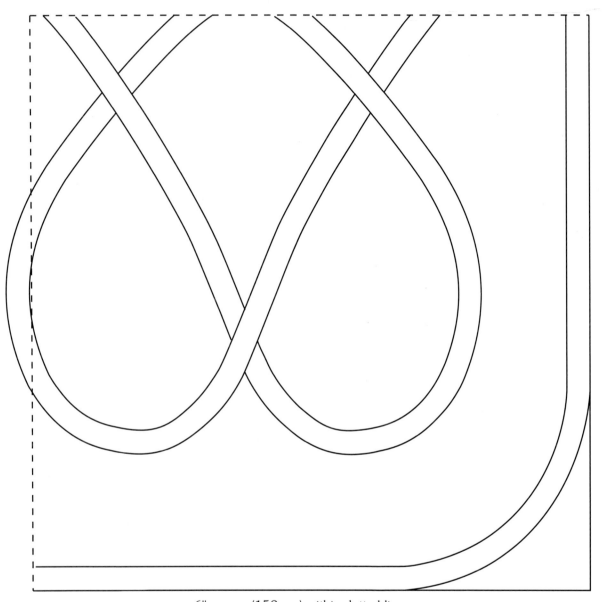

6" square (152mm) within dotted lines

Section #27

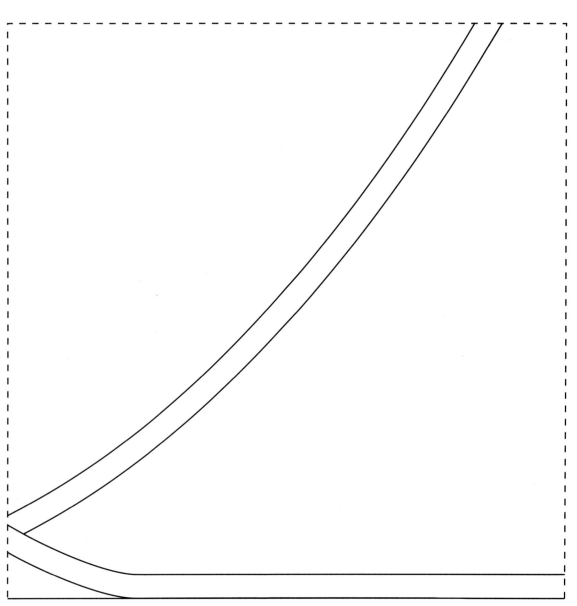

6" square (152mm)

Section #28

6" square (152mm)

Section #29

¼" (6mm)

1" (25mm)

¼" (6mm)

Section #30a – 1½" (38mm) Lattice

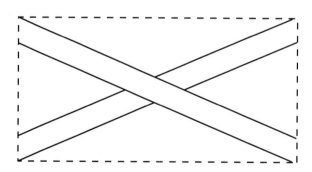

Section #30b – Lattice Intersection

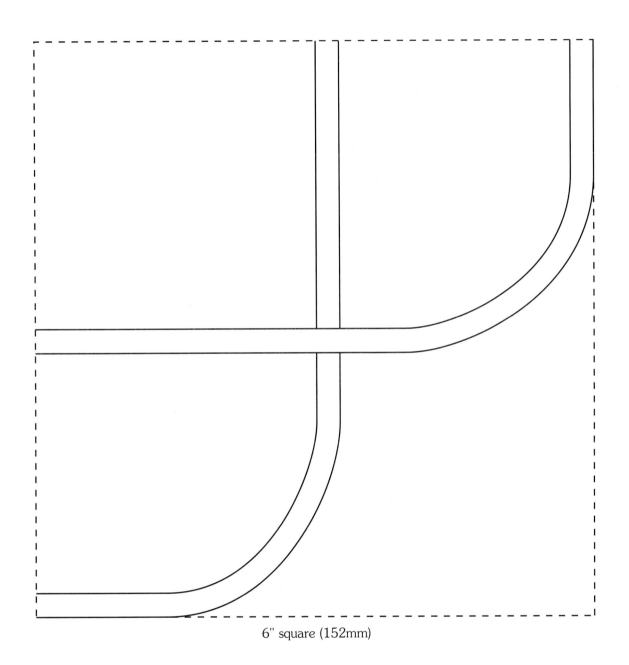

6" square (152mm)

Section #31 – 3" (76mm) Lattice Corner

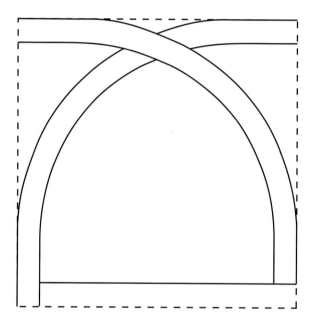

3" square (76mm)

Section #32 – Lattice Edge

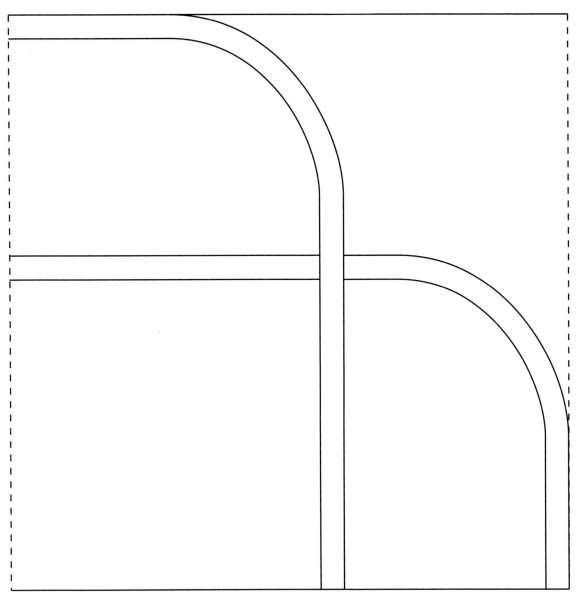

6" square (152mm)

Section #33 – Lattice
2¾" (70mm) lattice, center block corner.

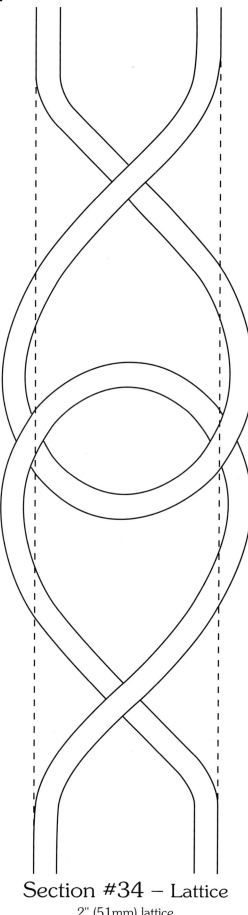

Section #34 – Lattice

2" (51mm) lattice

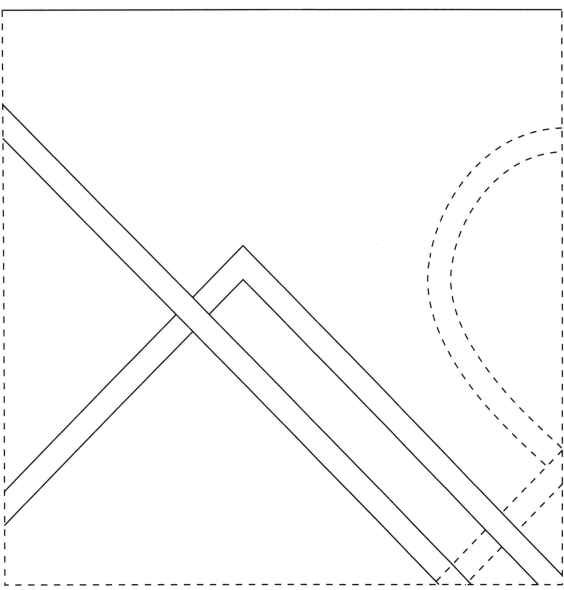

6" square (152mm)

Section #35
Dashed lines indicate where loop can be added to design.

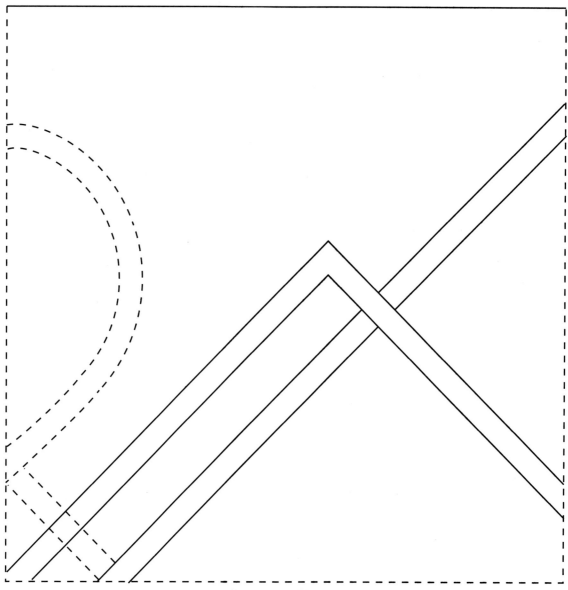

6" square (152mm)

Section #36

Dashed lines indicate where loop can be added to design.

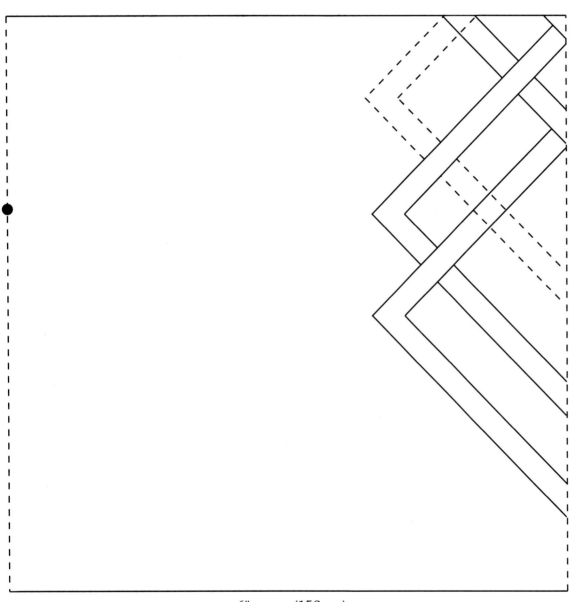

6" square (152mm)

Section #37

Dashed lines indicate where design can be modified, if using loop with Section #36.

Some intersections will need to change to accommodate added lines.

• Dot indicates where flower can be placed.

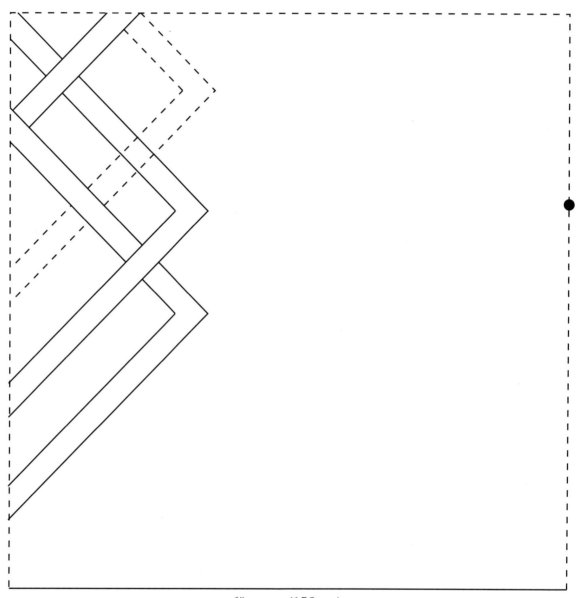

6" square (152mm)

Section #38

Dashed lines indicate where design can be modified, if using loop with Section #36.

Some intersections will need to change to accommodate added lines.

• Dot indicates where flower can be placed.

6" square (152mm)

Section #39

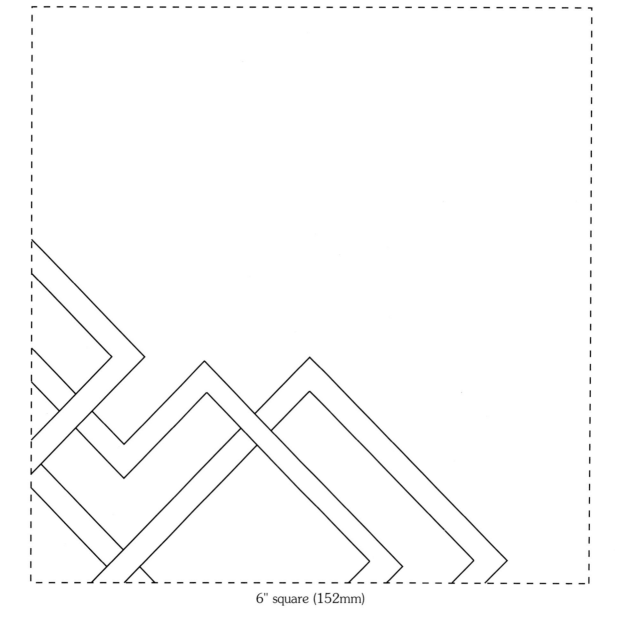

6" square (152mm)

Section #40

6" square (152mm)

Section #41

6" square (152mm)

Section #42

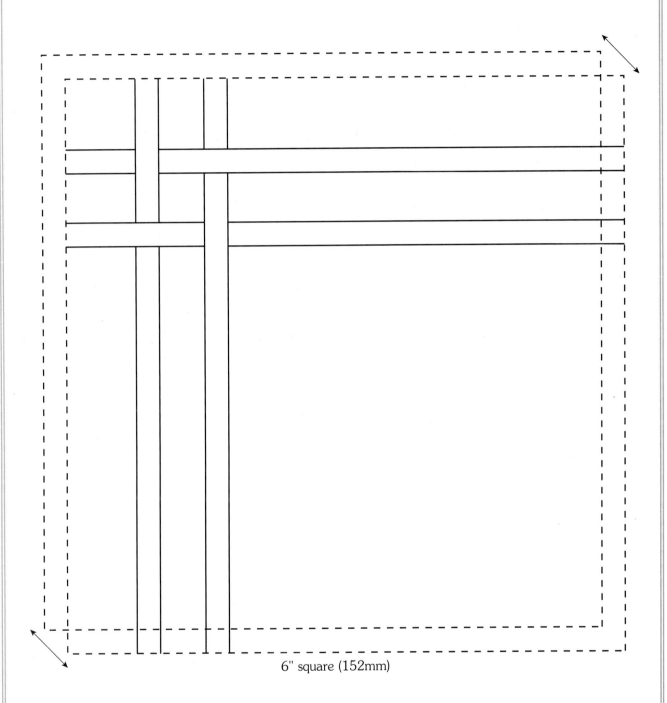

6" square (152mm)

Section #43

Shift 6" (305mm) square as needed to match connecting bias strips.

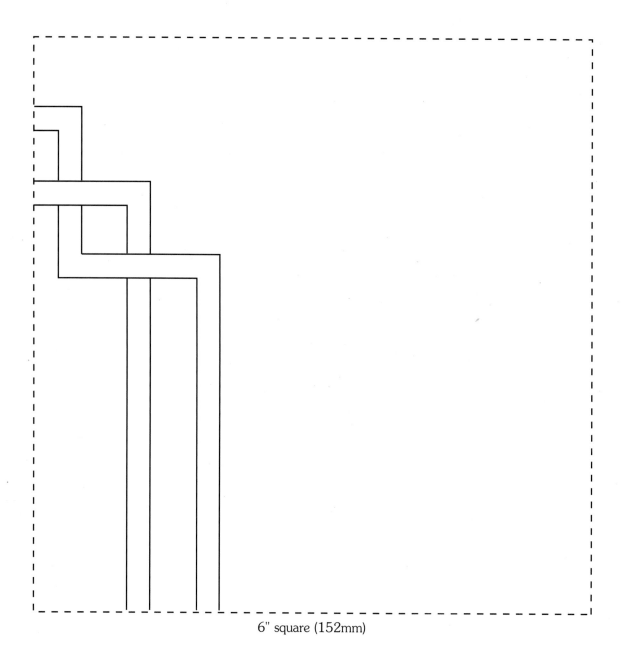

6" square (152mm)

Section #44

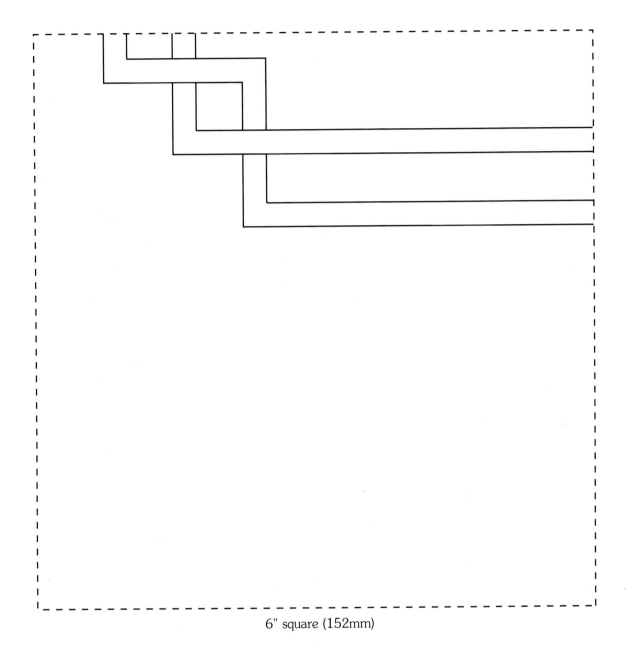

6" square (152mm)

Section #45

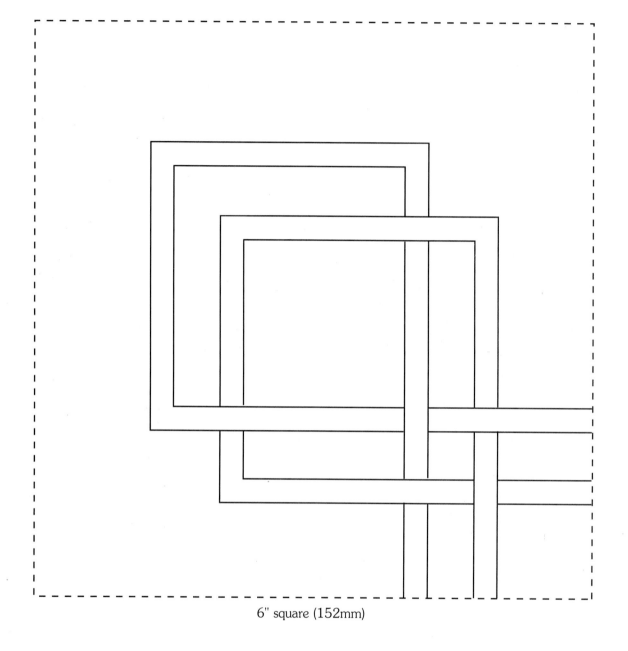

6" square (152mm)

Section #46

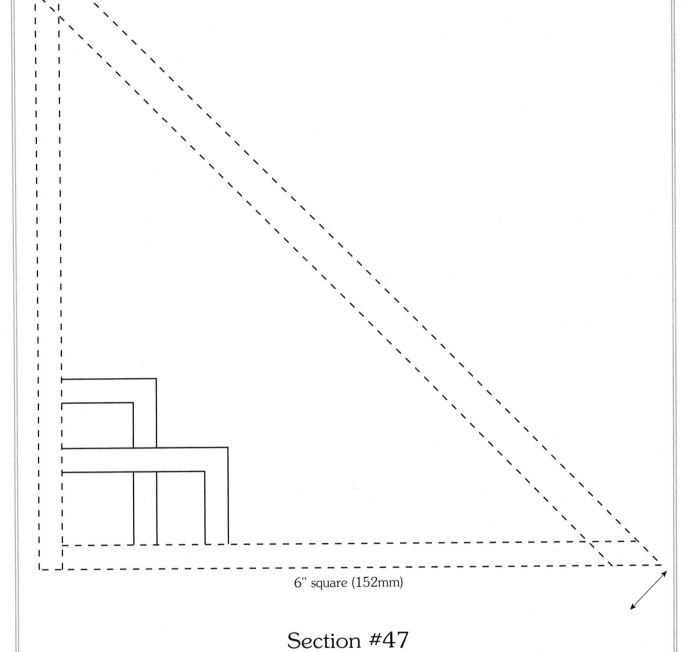

6" square (152mm)

Section #47

Shift triangle as needed to match connecting bias strips.

Section #48

6" square (152mm)

Section #49

B
6" square (152mm)

A

Section #50a – Celtic Rose Wreath
Rose appliqué was taken from Elly Sienkiewicz's block, #39 Albertine's Rose Climber.
Substitute another flower of your choice if pattern is unavailable.

A

B

6" square (152mm)

Section #50b – Celtic Rose Wreath

Rose appliqué was taken from Elly Sienkiewicz's block, #39 Albertine's Rose Climber.
Substitute another flower of your choice if pattern is unavailable.

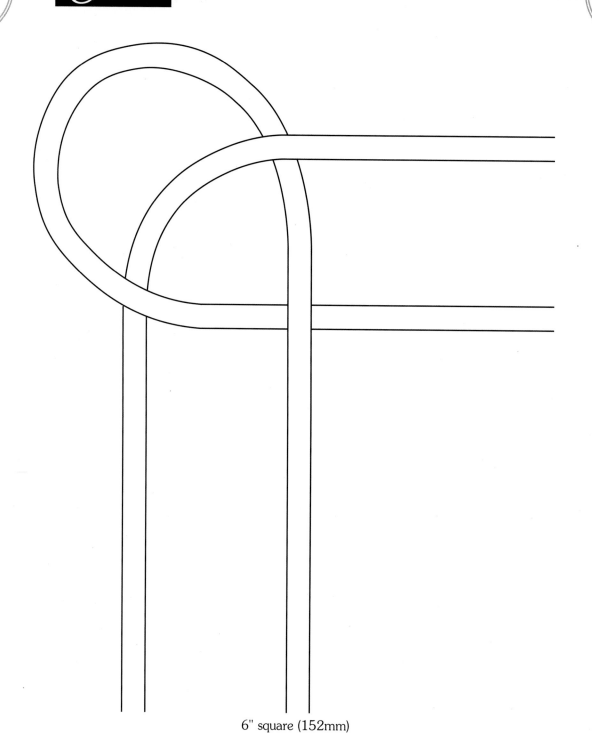

6" square (152mm)

Section #51

For lattice 2" (50mm) or 3" (76mm) border.

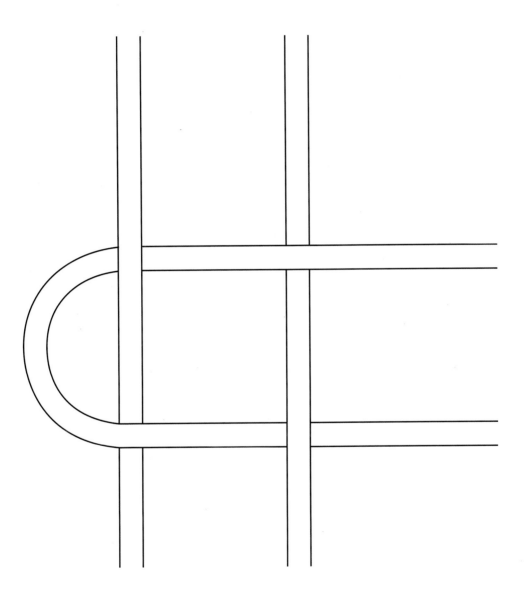

6" square (152mm)

Section #52
For lattice 2" (50mm) or 3" (76mm) border.

The Flower Patterns

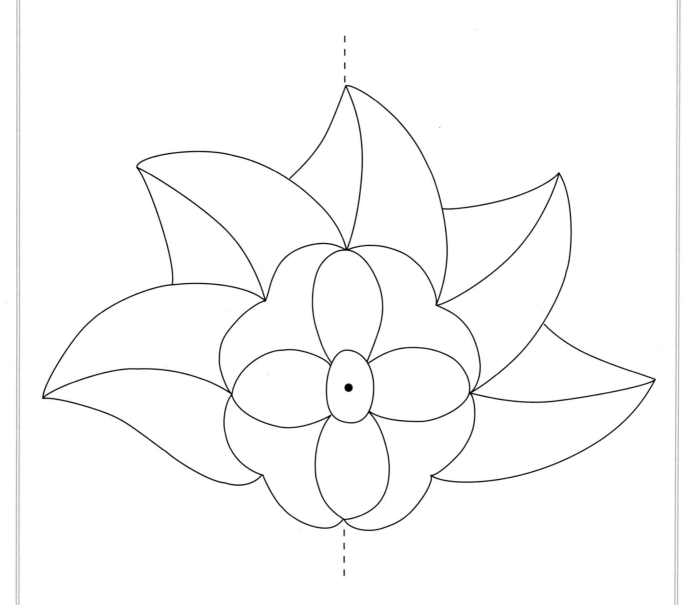

Flower #10

Mirror image when using for basket tops. Dashed lines should be matched to diagonal dashed lines on blocks.

• Dot indicates where flower is placed.

Patterns for Flowers #1–9 are given in my first book, so the flowers in this book begin with #10.

Flower #11

Dashed lines should be matched to diagonal dashed lines on blocks.

• Dot indicates where flower is placed.

Flower #12

Dashed lines should be matched to diagonal dashed lines on blocks.

• Dot indicates where flower is placed.

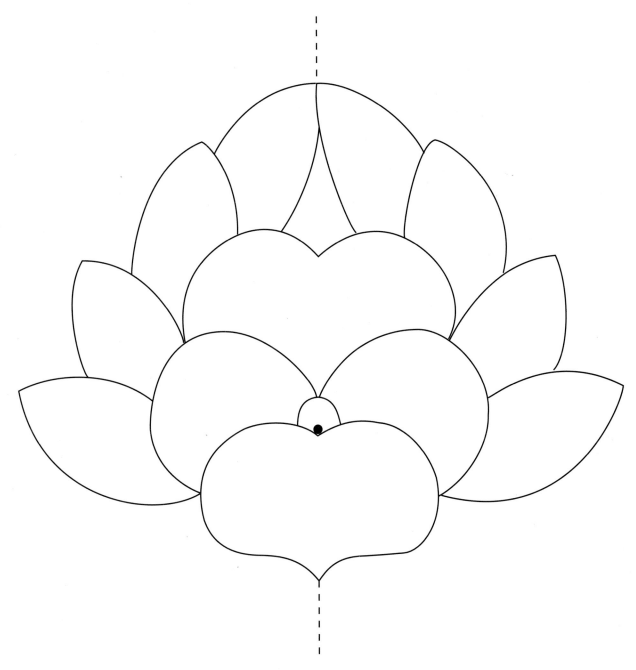

Flower #13

Dashed lines should be matched to diagonal dashed lines on blocks.

• Dot indicates where flower is placed.

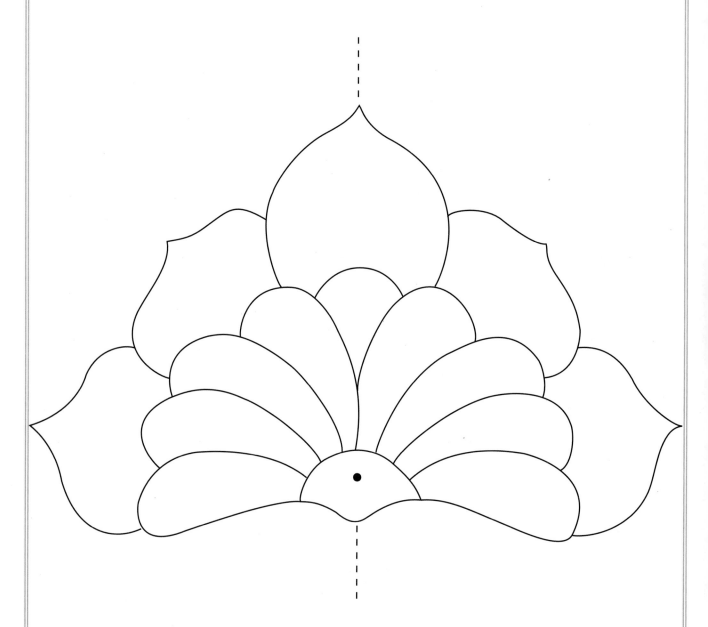

Flower #14

Dashed lines should be matched to diagonal dashed lines on blocks.

• Dot indicates where flower is placed.

Flower #15a

Dashed lines should be matched to diagonal dashed lines on blocks.

• Dot indicates where flower is placed.

Flower #15b

Flower #15c

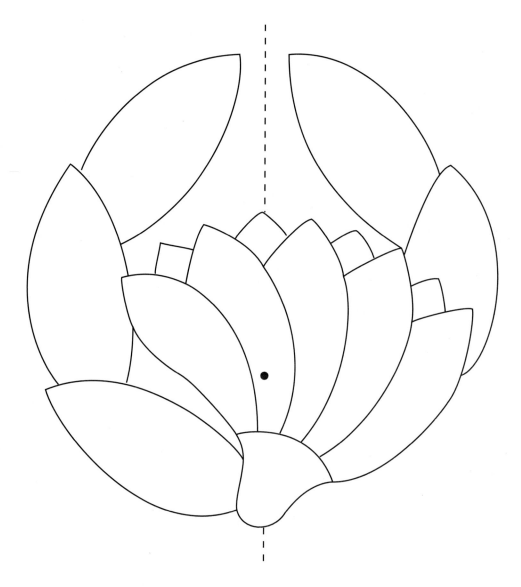

Flower #16

Mirror image when using for basket tops. Dashed lines should be matched to diagonal dashed lines on blocks.

• Dot indicates where flower is placed.

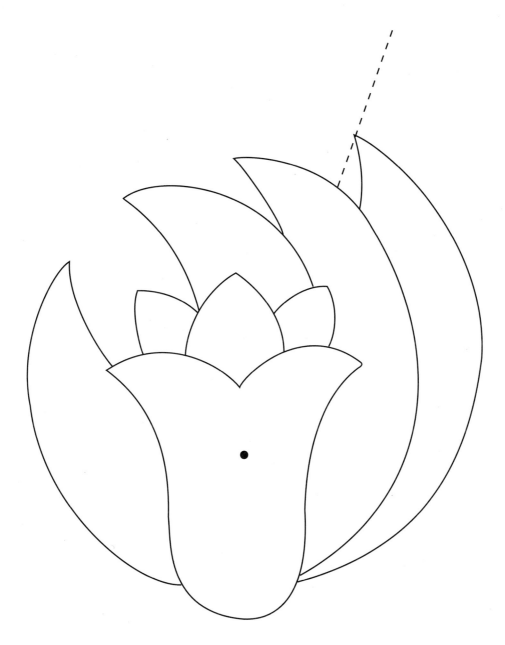

Flower #17

Mirror image when using for basket tops. Dashed lines should be matched to diagonal dashed lines on blocks.

• Dot indicates where flower is placed.

The Block Patterns

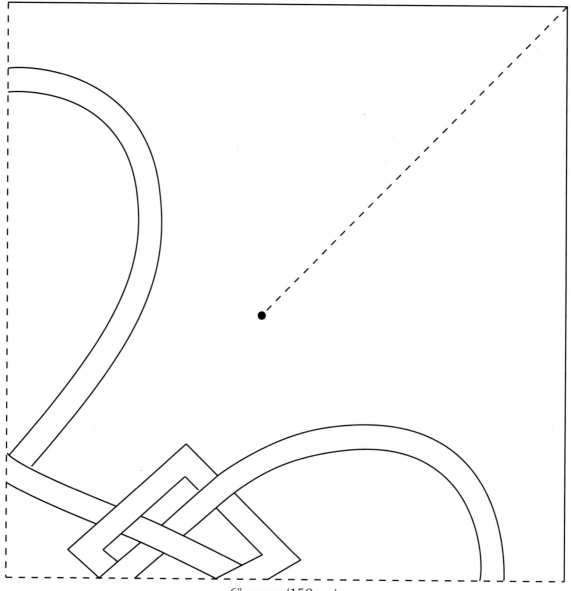

6" square (152mm)

Block #10a

Patterns for Blocks #1 – 9 are given in my first book *Celtic Style Floral Appliqué*; the blocks in this book begin with #10.

12" finished size (305mm)

¼ of design – copy 2 times, trim along dotted lines, follow assembly guide, match centers, then tape together.

Can use Flower #10 – 14, 16, 17

• Dot indicates where flower is to be placed and dashed line indicates the angle.

Block #10b	Block #10a
Block #10a	Block #10b

pattern guide

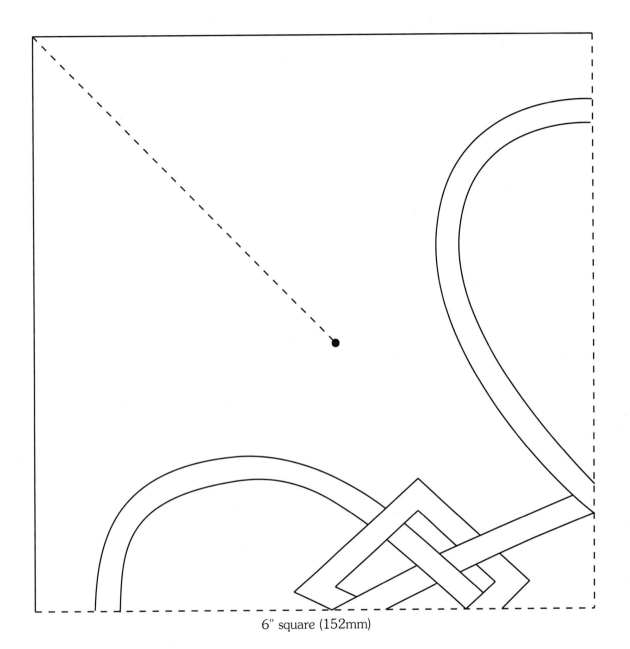

6" square (152mm)

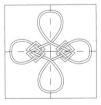

pattern guide

Block #10b

12" finished size (305mm)

¼ of design – copy 2 times, trim along dotted lines, follow assembly guide, match centers, then tape together.

Can use Flower #10 – 14, 16, 17

• Dot indicates where flower is to be placed and dashed line indicates the angle.

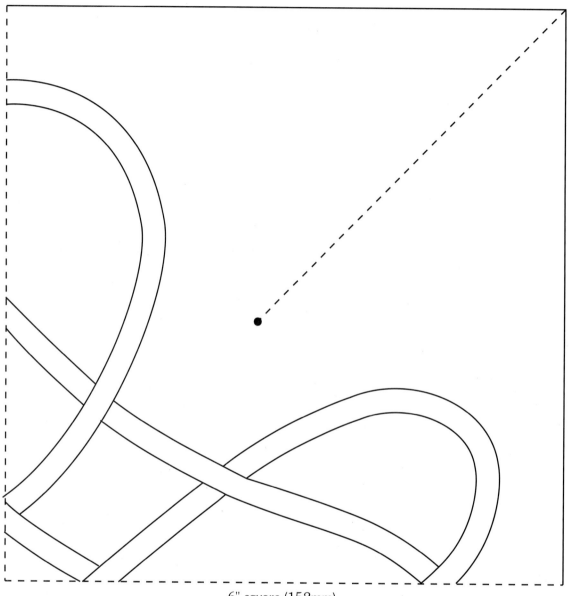

6" square (152mm)

Block #11b	Block #11a
Block #11a	Block #11b

pattern guide

Block #11a

12" finished size (305mm)

¼ of design – copy 2 times, trim along dotted lines, follow assembly guide, match centers, then tape together.

Can use Flower #10 – 15

• Dot indicates where flower is to be placed and dashed line indicates the angle.

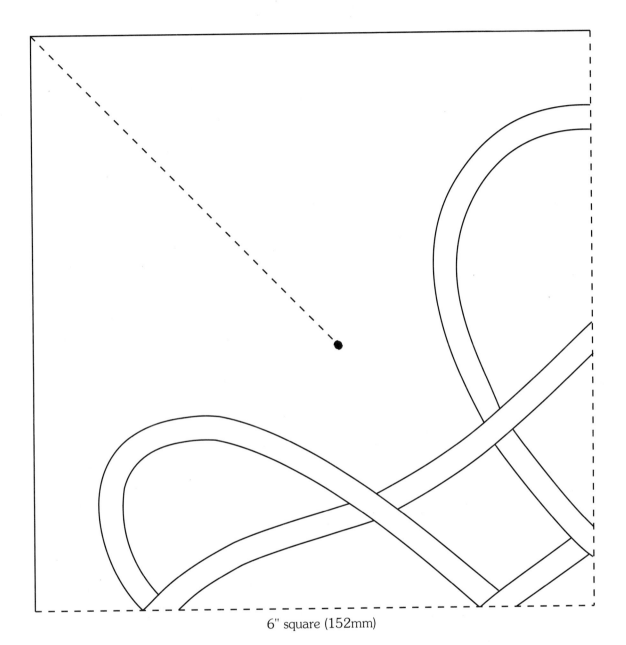

6" square (152mm)

pattern guide

Block #11b

12" finished size (305mm)

¼ of design – copy 2 times, trim along dotted lines, follow assembly guide, match centers, then tape together.

Can use Flower #10 – 15

• Dot indicates where flower is to be placed and dashed line indicates the angle.

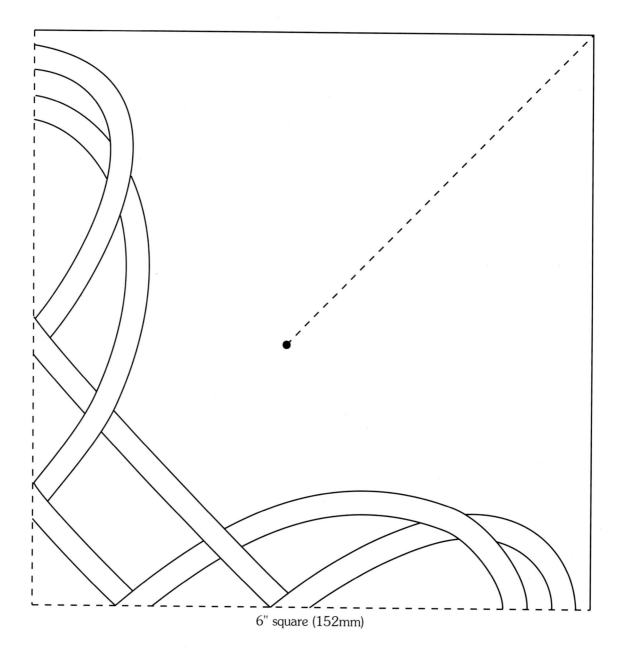

6" square (152mm)

pattern guide

Block #12

12" finished size (305mm)

¼ of design – copy 4 times, trim along dotted lines, match centers, then tape together.

Can use Flower #10 – 15

• Dot indicates where flower is to be placed and dashed line indicates the angle.

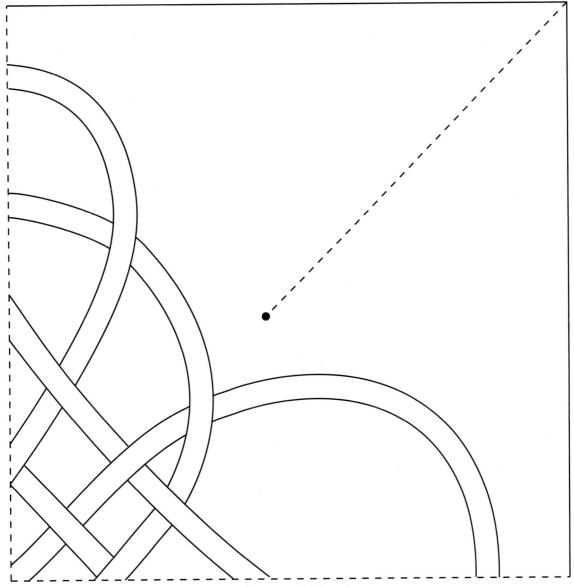

6" square (152mm)

Block #13b	Block #13a
Block #13a	Block #13b

pattern guide

Block #13a

12" finished size (305mm)

¼ of design – copy 2 times, trim along dotted lines, follow assembly guide, match centers, then tape together.

Can use Flower #11, 12

• Dot indicates where flower is to be placed and dashed line indicates the angle.

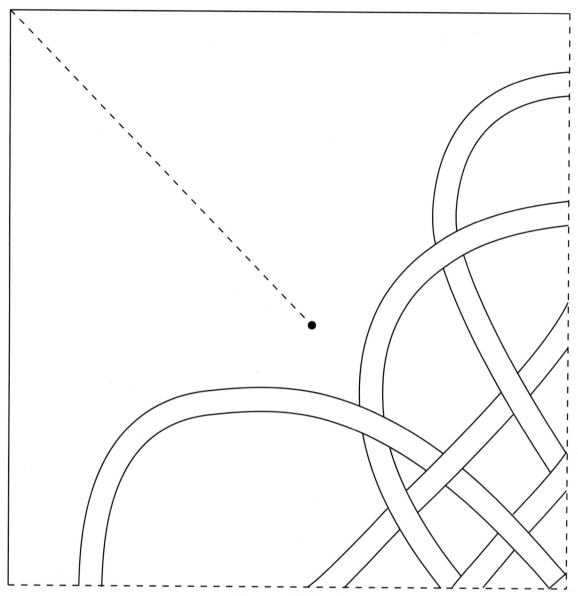

6" square (152mm)

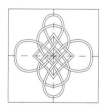

pattern guide

Block #13b

12" finished size (305mm)

¼ of design – copy 2 times, trim along dotted lines, follow assembly guide, match centers, then tape together.

Can use Flower #11, 12

• Dot indicates where flower is to be placed and dashed line indicates the angle.

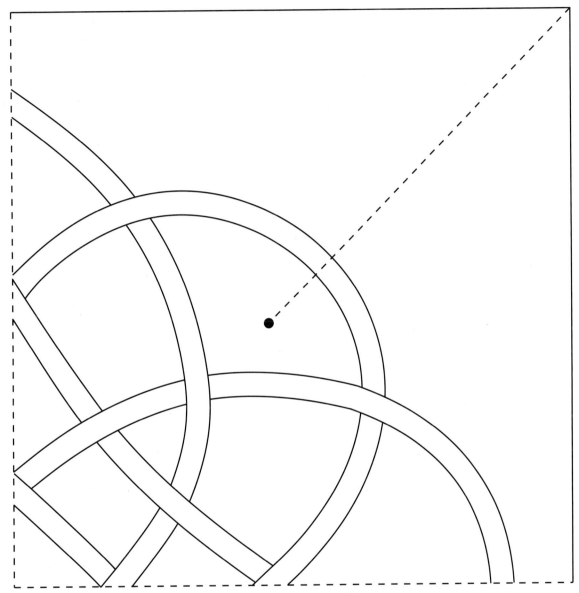

6" square (152mm)

Block #14b	Block #14a
Block #14a	Block #14b

pattern guide

Block #14a

12" finished size (305mm)

¼ of design – copy 2 times, trim along dotted lines, follow assembly guide, match centers, then tape together.

Can use Flower #14, 15

• Dot indicates where flower is to be placed and dashed line indicates the angle.

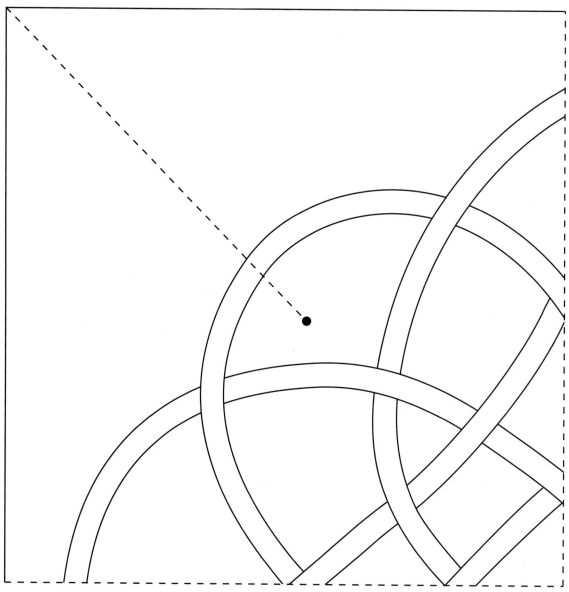

6" square (152mm)

pattern guide

Block #14b

12" finished size (305mm)

¼ of design – copy 2 times, trim along dotted lines, follow assembly guide, match centers, then tape together.

Can use Flower #14, 15

• Dot indicates where flower is to be placed and dashed line indicates the angle.

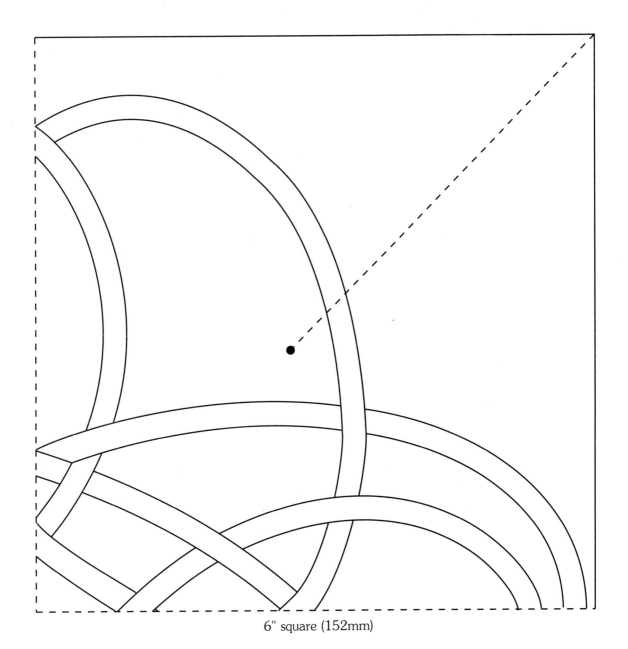

6" square (152mm)

Block #15b	Block #15a
Block #15a	Block #15b

pattern guide

Block #15a

12" finished size (305mm)

¼ of design – copy 2 times, trim along dotted lines, follow assembly guide, match centers, then tape together.

Can use Flower #15

• Dot indicates where flower is to be placed and dashed line indicates the angle.

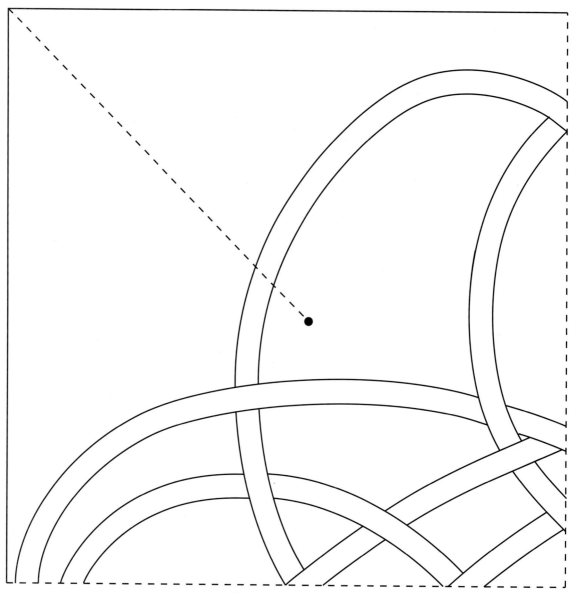

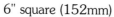

6" square (152mm)

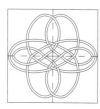

pattern guide

Block #15b

12" finished size (305mm)

¼ of design – copy 2 times, trim along dotted lines, follow assembly guide, match centers, then tape together.

Can use Flower #15

• Dot indicates where flower is to be placed and dashed line indicates the angle.

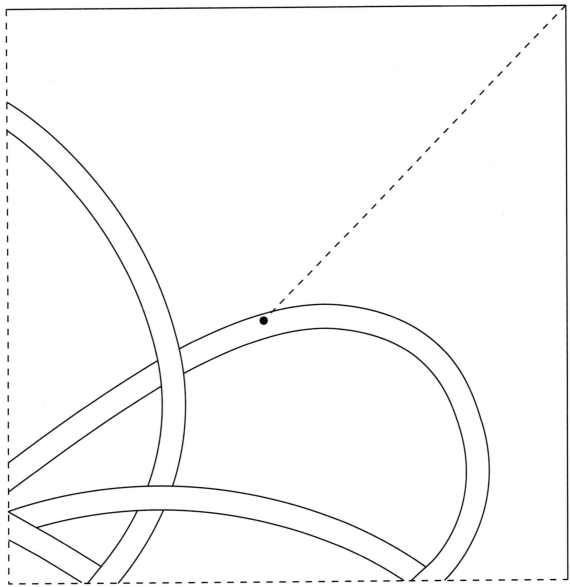

6" square (152mm)

Block #16b	Block #16a
Block #16a	Block #16b

pattern guide

Block #16a

12" finished size (305mm)

¼ of design – copy 2 times, trim along dotted lines, follow assembly guide, match centers, then tape together.

Can use Flower #15

• Dot indicates where flower is to be placed and dashed line indicates the angle.

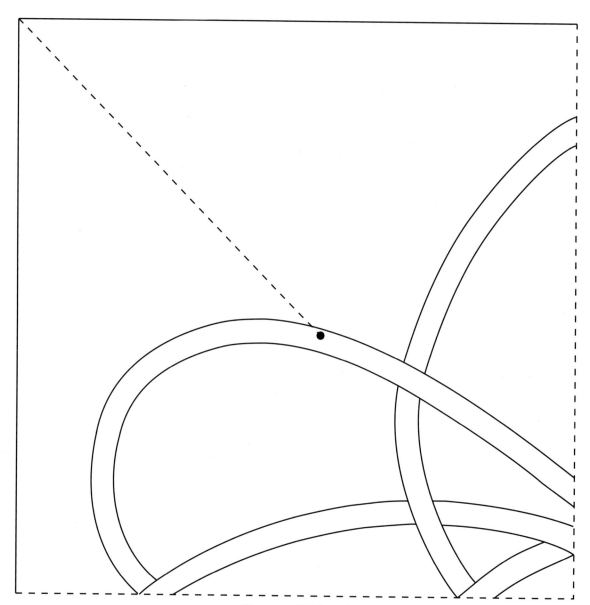

6" square (152mm)

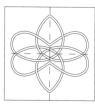

pattern guide

Block #16b

12" finished size (305mm)

¼ of design – copy 2 times, trim along dotted lines, follow assembly guide, match centers, then tape together.

Can use Flower #15

• Dot indicates where flower is to be placed and dashed line indicates the angle.

The Basket Patterns

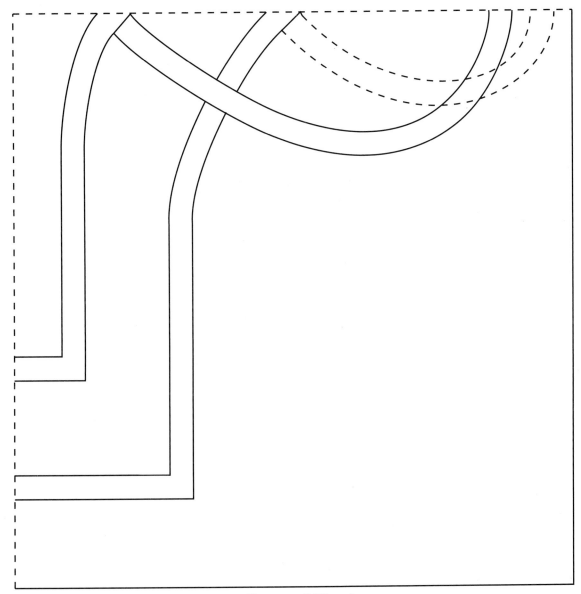

6" square (152mm)

Basket #1a

12" finished size (305mm)

¼ of design – copy 2 times, trim along dotted lines, follow assembly guide, match centers, then tape together.

Works with Block #1 (CSFA)

Works with Block #12 (loops added)

Works with Block #13 (miter center strip)

Works with Block #15 (loops added)

Dashed lines indicate modification to fit some blocks.

Basket #1a	Basket #1b
Basket #1b	Basket #1a

pattern guide

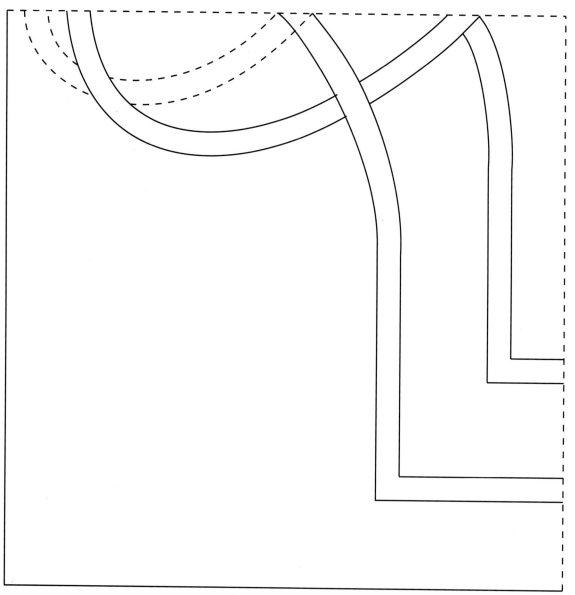

6" square (152mm)

Basket #1b

12" finished size (305mm)

¼ of design – copy 2 times, trim along dotted lines, follow assembly guide, match centers, then tape together.

Works with Block #1 (CSFA)

Works with Block #12 (loops added)

Works with Block #13 (miter center strip)

Works with Block #15 (loops added)

Dashed lines indicate modification to fit some blocks.

pattern guide

6" square (152mm)

Basket #2a

12" finished size (305mm)

¼ of design – copy 2 times, trim along dotted lines, follow assembly guide, match centers, then tape together.

Works with Block #2 (CSFA)

Works with Block #11

Works with Block #16

Basket #2a	Basket #2b
Basket #2b	Basket #2a

pattern guide

6" square (152mm)

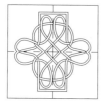

pattern guide

Basket #2b

12" finished size (305mm)

¼ of design – copy 2 times, trim along dotted lines, follow assembly guide, match centers, then tape together.

Works with Block #2 (CSFA)

Works with Block #11

Works with Block #16

6" square (152mm)

Basket #3a

12" finished size (305mm)

¼ of design – copy 2 times, trim along dotted lines, follow assembly guide, match centers, then tape together.

Works with Block #3 (CSFA)

Works with Block #12, 15

Works with Block #10, 14 (loops added)

Works with Block #13 (loops added and miter center strips)

Basket #3a	Basket #3b
Basket #3b	Basket #3a

pattern guide

6" square (152mm)

Basket #3b

12" finished size (305mm)

¼ of design – copy 2 times, trim along dotted lines, follow assembly guide, match centers, then tape together.

Works with Block #3 (CSFA)

Works with Block #12, 15

Works with Block #10, 14 (loops added)

Works with Block #13 (loops added and miter center strips)

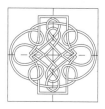

pattern guide

6" square (152mm)

Basket #4a

12" finished size (305mm)

¼ of design – copy 2 times, trim along dotted lines, follow assembly guide, match centers, then tape together.

Works with Block #4 (CSFA)

Basket #4a	Basket #4b
Basket #4b	Basket #4a

pattern guide

6" square (152mm)

Basket #4b

12" finished size (305mm)

¼ of design – copy 2 times, trim along dotted lines, follow assembly guide, match centers, then tape together.

Works with Block #4 (CSFA)

pattern guide

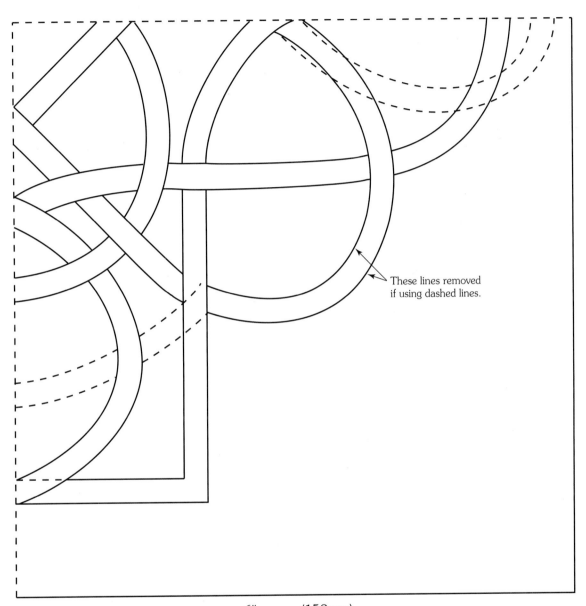

These lines removed
if using dashed lines.

6" square (152mm)

Basket #5a

12" finished size (305mm)

¼ of design – copy 2 times, trim along dotted lines, follow assembly guide, match centers, then tape together.

Works with Block #5 (CSFA)

Works with Block #10, 14

Works with Block #12, 15 (with some loops added and some removed)

Dashed lines indicate modification to fit some blocks.

Basket #5a	Basket #5b
Basket #5b	Basket #5a

pattern guide

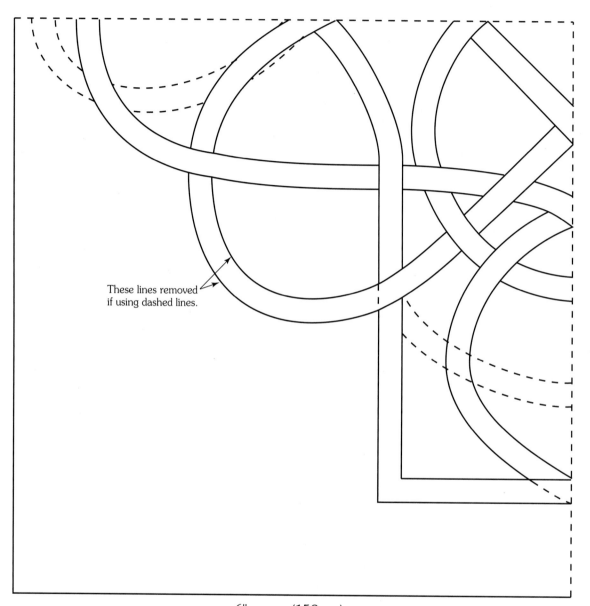

These lines removed
if using dashed lines.

6" square (152mm)

Basket #5b

12" finished size (305mm)

¼ of design – copy 2 times, trim along dotted lines, follow assembly guide, match centers, then tape together.

Works with Block #5 (CSFA)

Works with Block #10, 14

Works with Block #12, 15 (with some loops added and some removed)

Dashed lines indicate modification to fit some blocks.

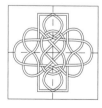

pattern guide

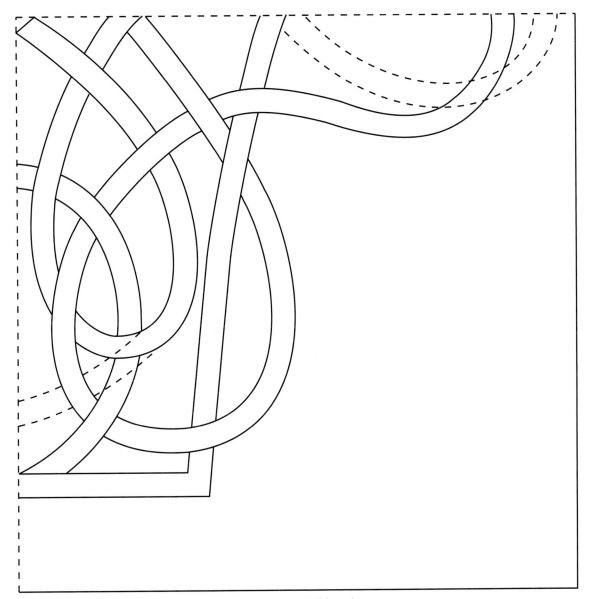

6" square (152mm)

Basket #6a

12" finished size (305mm)

¼ of design – copy 2 times, trim along dotted lines, follow assembly guide, match centers, then tape together.

Dashed lines indicate modification, if necessary to match blocks or fit basket into lattice border.

Basket #6a	Basket #6b
Basket #6b	Basket #6a

pattern guide

Works with Block #6, 7, 8, 9 (CSFA)

Works with Block #13

Works with Block #12, 15 (add loops and miter center strips of basket)

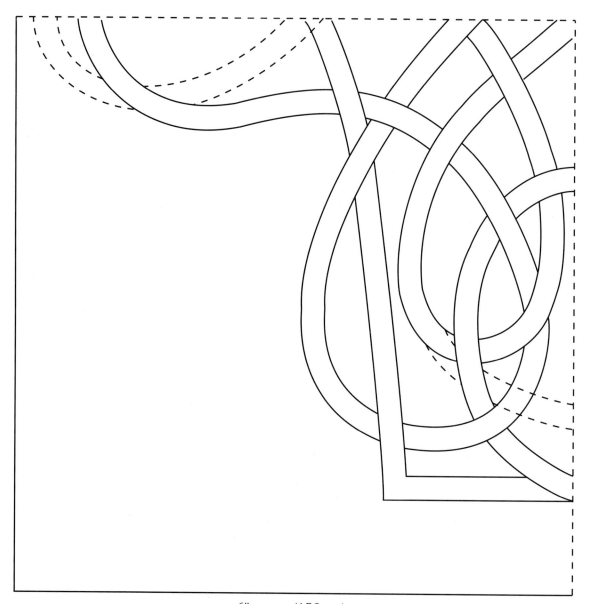

6" square (152mm)

Basket #6b

12" finished size (305mm)

¼ of design – copy 2 times, trim along dotted lines, follow assembly guide, match centers, then tape together.

Dashed lines indicate modification, if necessary to match blocks or fit basket to lattice border.

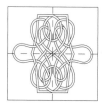

pattern guide

Works with Block #6, 7, 8, 9 (CSFA)

Works with Block #13

Works with Block #12, 15 (add loops and miter center strips of basket)

6" square (152mm)

Basket #7a

12" finished size (305mm)

¼ of design – copy 2 times, trim along dotted lines, follow assembly guide, match centers, then tape together.

Works with Block #6, 7, 8, 9 (CSFA)

Works with Block #13

Works with Block #12, 15 (add loops and miter center strips of basket)

Dashed lines indicate modification to fit some blocks.

Basket #7a	Basket #7b
Basket #7b	Basket #7a

pattern guide

6" square (152mm)

Basket #7b

12" finished size (305mm)

¼ of design – copy 2 times, trim along dotted lines, follow assembly guide, match centers, then tape together.

Works with Block #6, 7, 8, 9 (CSFA)

Works with Block #13

Works with Block #12, 15 (add loops and miter center strips of basket)

Dashed lines indicate modification to fit some blocks.

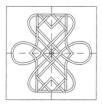

pattern guide

6" square (152mm)

Basket #8a

12" finished size (305mm)

¼ of design – copy 2 times, trim along dotted lines, follow assembly guide, match centers, then tape together.

Works with Block #6, 7, 8, 9 (CSFA)

Works with Block #13

Works with Block #12, 15 (add loops and miter center strips of basket)

Dashed lines indicate modification to fit some blocks.

Basket #8a	Basket #8b
Basket #8b	Basket #8a

pattern guide

6" square (152mm)

Basket #8b

12" finished size (305mm)

¼ of design – copy 2 times, trim along dotted lines, follow assembly guide, match centers, then tape together.

Works with Block #6, 7, 8, 9 (CSFA)

Works with Block #13

Works with Block #12, 15 (add loops and miter center strips of basket)

Dashed lines indicate modification to fit some blocks.

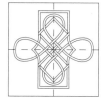

pattern guide

6" square (152mm)

Basket #9a

12" finished size (305mm)

¼ of design – copy 2 times, trim along dotted lines, follow assembly guide, match centers, then tape together.

Works with Block #6, 7, 8, 9 (CSFA)

Works with Block #13

Works with Block #12, 15 (add loops and miter center strips of basket)

Dashed lines indicate modification to fit some blocks.

Basket #9a	Basket #9b
Basket #9b	Basket #9a

pattern guide

6" square (152mm)

Basket #9b

12" finished size (305mm)

¼ of design – copy 2 times, trim along dotted lines, follow assembly guide, match centers, then tape together.

Works with Block #6, 7, 8, 9 (CSFA)

Works with Block #13

Works with Block #12, 15 (add loops and miter center strips of basket)

Dashed lines indicate modification to fit some blocks.

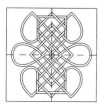

pattern guide

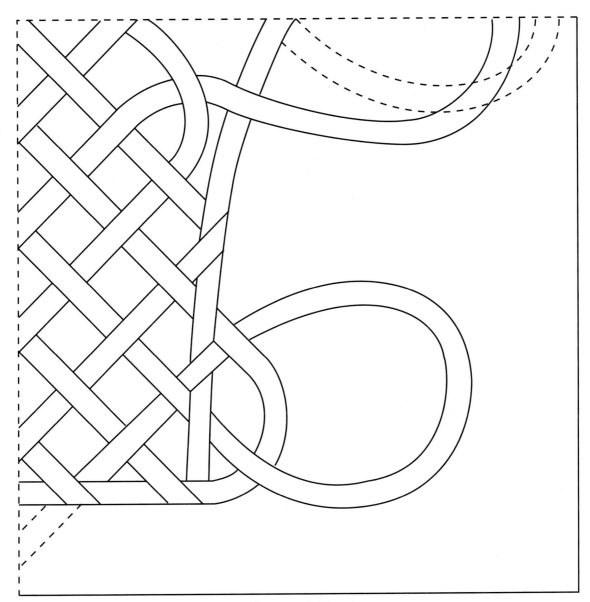

6" square (152mm)

Basket #10a

12" finished size (305mm)

¼ of design – copy 2 times, trim along dotted lines, follow assembly guide, match centers, then tape together.

Works with Block #6, 7, 8, 9 (CSFA)

Works with Block #13

Works with Block #12, 15 (add loops and miter center strips of basket)

Dashed lines indicate modification to fit some blocks.

Basket #10a	Basket #10b
Basket #10b	Basket #10a

pattern guide

6" square (152mm)

Basket #10b

12" finished size (305mm)

¼ of design – copy 2 times, trim along dotted lines, follow assembly guide, match centers, then tape together.

Works with Block #6, 7, 8, 9 (CSFA)

Works with Block #13

Works with Block #12, 15 (add loops and miter center strips of basket)

Dashed lines indicate modification to fit some blocks.

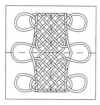

pattern guide

6" square (152mm)

Basket #11a

12" finished size (305mm)

¼ of design – copy 2 times, trim along dotted lines, follow assembly guide, match centers, then tape together.

Works with Block #1 (CSFA)

Works with Block #13 (miter center strips)

Basket #11a	Basket #11b
Basket #11b	Basket #11a

pattern guide

6" square (152mm)

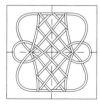

pattern guide

Basket #11b

12" finished size (305mm)

¼ of design – copy 2 times, trim along dotted lines, follow assembly guide, match centers, then tape together.

Works with Block #1 (CSFA)

Works with Block #13 (miter center strips)

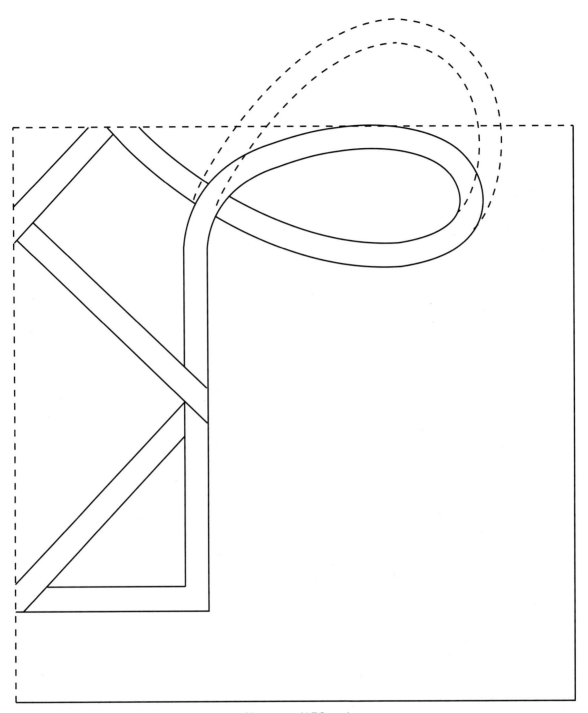

6" square (152mm)

Basket #12a	Basket #12b
Basket #12b	Basket #12a

pattern guide

Basket #12a

12" finished size (305mm)

¼ of design – copy 2 times, trim along dotted lines, follow assembly guide, match centers, then tape together.

Dashed lines indicate modification, if necessary

Works with Block #4 (CSFA)

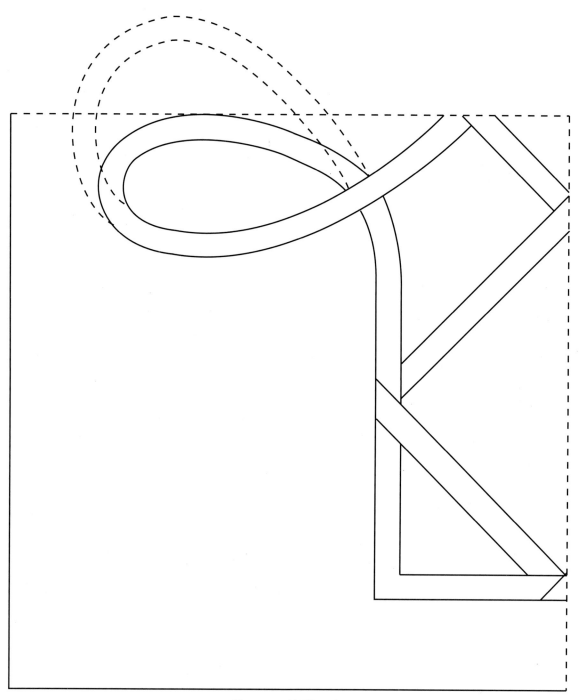

6" square (152mm)

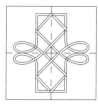

pattern guide

Basket #12b

12" finished size (305mm)

¼ of design – copy 2 times, trim along dotted lines, follow assembly guide, match centers, then tape together.

Dashed lines indicate modification, if necessary

Works with Block #4 (CSFA)

BIBLIOGRAPHY

Magaret, Pat Maizner and Slusser, Donna Ingram, *Watercolor Quilts,* That Patchwork Place, Bothell, WA, 1993.

Rose, Scarlett, *Celtic Style Floral Appliqué*, American Quilter's Society, Paducah, KY, 1995.

Sienkiewicz, Elly, *Baltimore Album Quilts*, C&T Publishing, Lafayette, CA, 1990.

SOURCES

For marbled fabrics by Marjorie Lee Bevis:

Marbled Fabric and Accessories
325 4th St.
Petaluma, CA 94952
707-762-7514
FAX: 707-762-2548
E-mail: MARBLEFAB@aol.com

For metallic threads:

Nancy's Notions, LTD
P.O. Box 683
Beaver Dam, WI 53916-0683
order phone 1-800-833-0690
FAX: 1-800-255-8119
Web site: http://www.nancysnotions.com

For metal bias bars:

Celtic Design Co.
P.O. Box 2643
Sunnyvale, CA 94087-0643
phone or FAX: 408-735-8049

For Hobbs Thermore® batting:

Hancock's
3841 Hinkleville Rd.
Exit 4 off I 24
Paducah, KY 42001
24 hrs. 1-800-626-2723
FAX: 502-442-2164
E-mail: DSingBear@aol.com

ABOUT THE AUTHOR

Born and raised in northern California, Scarlett Rose started quilting in 1976 while in high school. She began designing her own quilt patterns in the early 1980s. After joining a local quilt group in 1982 and discovering the wide variety of quilt shows and competitions, she began entering her quilts in many contests, winning numerous awards. One of her quilts, STAR BRIGHT, won honorable mention in a challenge contest and was published in 1992 by *Quilt World* magazine in a special issue, "Blue Ribbon Quilts." Encouraged by the interest shown in her designs and requests for patterns, Scarlett submitted two quilts, AUTUMN LEAVES and STARS AND THEIR FANS, to Oxmoor House. Patterns for both were published in *Great American Quilts 1993*. After attending the American Quilter's Society quilt show in Paducah in 1993, she submitted a book proposal which was accepted and became her first book, *Celtic Style Floral Appliqué*, published in 1995.

Scarlett has an array of designs planned for future books, some continuing in the Celtic style, as well as patterns for different kinds of quilts. She also designs wearable art, using the skills and techniques she has learned from quilting classes and books, combined with sewing almost all her own clothing since age 12. This knowledge has been merged with her own heritage, leading to special clothing designs, such as the kimono she sewed for her wedding on May 10, 1997. She used parts of a Japanese wedding kimono in creating her own version of a wedding dress that reflects her personal style.

Since 1986 she has taught classes on basic and Celtic appliqué, and lectured on Celtic appliqué, wearable art: a Japanese theme wedding, friendship quilts, and a retrospective of her quilting evolution.

AQS Books on Quilts

This is only a partial listing of the books on quilts that are available from the American Quilter's Society. AQS books are known the world over for their timely topics, clear writing, beautiful color photographs, and accurate illustrations and patterns. The following books are available from your local bookseller, quilt shop, or public library. If you are unable to locate certain titles in your area, you may order by mail from the AMERICAN QUILTER'S SOCIETY, P.O. Box 3290, Paducah, KY 42002-3290. Add $2.00 for postage for the first book ordered and 40¢ for each additional book. Include item number, title, and price when ordering. Allow 14 to 21 days for delivery. Customers with Visa, MasterCard, or Discover may phone in orders from 7:00–5:00 CST, Monday–Friday, Toll Free 1-800-626-5420.

4595	**Above & Beyond Basics**, Karen Kay Buckley	$18.95
2282	**Adapting Architectural Details for Quilts**, Carol Wagner	$12.95
4813	**Addresses & Birthdays**, compiled by Klaudeen Hansen **(HB)**	$14.95
4543	**American Quilt Blocks: 50 Patterns for 50 States**, Beth Summers	$16.95
4696	**Amish Kinder Komforts**, Bettina Havig	$14.95
4829	**Anita Shackelford: Surface Textures**, Anita Shackelford **(HB)**	$24.95
4899	**Appliqué Paper Greetings**, Elly Sienkiewicz **(HB)**	$24.95
3790	**Appliqué Patterns from Native American Beadwork Designs**, Dr. Joyce Mori	$14.95
2099	**Ask Helen: More About Quilting Designs**, Helen Squire	$14.95
2207	**Award-Winning Quilts: 1985-1987**	$24.95
2354	**Award-Winning Quilts: 1988-1989**	$24.95
3425	**Award-Winning Quilts: 1990-1991**	$24.95
3791	**Award-Winning Quilts: 1992-1993**	$24.95
4830	**Baskets: Celtic Style**, Scarlett Rose	$19.95
4832	**A Batch of Patchwork**, May T. Miller & Susan B. Burton	$18.95
4593	**Blossoms by the Sea: Making Ribbon Flowers for Quilts**, Faye Labanaris	$24.95
4898	**Borders & Finishing Touches**, Bonnie K. Browning	$16.95
4697	**Caryl Bryer Fallert: A Spectrum of Quilts, 1983-1995**, Caryl Bryer Fallert	$24.95
4626	**Celtic Geometric Quilts**, Camille Remme	$16.95
3926	**Celtic Style Floral Appliqué**, Scarlett Rose	$14.95
2208	**Classic Basket Quilts**, Elizabeth Porter & Marianne Fons	$16.95
2355	**Creative Machine Art**, Sharee Dawn Roberts	$24.95
4818	**Dear Helen, Can You Tell Me?** Helen Squire	$15.95
3399	**Dye Painting!** Ann Johnston	$19.95
4814	**Encyclopedia of Designs for Quilting**, Phyllis D. Miller **(HB)**	$34.95
3468	**Encyclopedia of Pieced Quilt Patterns**, compiled by Barbara Brackman	$34.95
3846	**Fabric Postcards**, Judi Warren	$22.95
4594	**Firm Foundations**, Jane Hall & Dixie Haywood	$18.95
4900	**Four Blocks Continued…**, Linda Giesler Carlson	$16.95
2381	**From Basics to Binding**, Karen Kay Buckley	$16.95
4526	**Gatherings: America's Quilt Heritage**, Kathlyn F. Sullivan	$34.95
2097	**Heirloom Miniatures**, Tina M. Gravatt	$9.95
4628	**Helen's Guide to quilting in the 21st century**, Helen Squire	$16.95
1906	**Irish Chain Quilts: A Workbook of Irish Chains**, Joyce B. Peaden	$14.95
3784	**Jacobean Appliqué: Book I, "Exotica,"** Campbell & Ayars	$18.95
4544	**Jacobean Appliqué: Book II, "Romantica,"** Campbell & Ayars	$18.95
3904	**The Judge's Task**, Patricia J. Morris	$19.95
4751	**Liberated Quiltmaking**, Gwen Marston **(HB)**	$24.95
4897	**Lois Smith's Machine Quiltmaking**, Lois Smith	$19.95
4523	**Log Cabin Quilts: New Quilts from an Old Favorite**	$14.95
4545	**Log Cabin with a Twist**, Barbara T. Kaempfer	$18.95
4815	*Love to Quilt:* **Bears, Bears, Bears**, Karen Kay Buckley	$14.95
4833	*Love to Quilt:* **Broderie Perse: The Elegant Quilt**, Barbara W. Barber	$14.95
4598	*Love to Quilt:* **Men's Vests**, Alexandra Capadalis Dupré	$14.95
4816	*Love to Quilt:* **Necktie Sampler Blocks**, Janet B. Elwin	$14.95
4753	*Love to Quilt:* **Penny Squares**, Willa Baranowski	$12.95
4911	**Mariner's Compass Quilts: New Quilts from an Old Favorite**	$16.95
4752	**Miniature Quilts: Connecting New & Old Worlds**, Tina M. Gravatt	$14.95
4514	**Mola Techniques for Today's Quilters**, Charlotte Patera	$18.95
3330	**More Projects and Patterns**, Judy Florence	$18.95
1981	**Nancy Crow: Quilts and Influences**, Nancy Crow	$29.95
3331	**Nancy Crow: Work in Transition**, Nancy Crow	$12.95
4828	**Nature, Design & Silk Ribbons**, Cathy Grafton	$18.95
3332	**New Jersey Quilts**, The Heritage Quilt Project of New Jersey	$29.95
3927	**New Patterns from Old Architecture**, Carol Wagner	$12.95
2153	**No Dragons on My Quilt**, Jean Ray Laury	$12.95
4627	**Ohio Star Quilts: New Quilts from an Old Favorite**	$16.95
3469	**Old Favorites in Miniature**, Tina Gravatt	$15.95
4831	**Optical Illusions for Quilters**, Karen Combs	$22.95
4515	**Paint and Patches: Painting on Fabrics with Pigment**, Vicki L. Johnson	$18.95
4513	**Plaited Patchwork**, Shari Cole	$19.95
3928	**Precision Patchwork for Scrap Quilts**, Jeannette Tousley Muir	$12.95
4779	**Protecting Your Quilts: A Guide for Quilt Owners, Second Edition**	$6.95
4542	**A Quilted Christmas**, edited by Bonnie Browning	$18.95
2380	**Quilter's Registry**, Lynne Fritz	$9.95
3467	**Quilting Patterns from Native American Designs**, Dr. Joyce Mori	$12.95
3470	**Quilting with Style**, Gwen Marston & Joe Cunningham	$24.95
2284	**Quiltmaker's Guide: Basics & Beyond**, Carol Doak	$19.95
4918	**Quilts by Paul D. Pilgrim: Blending the Old & the New**, Gerald E. Roy	$16.95
2257	*Quilts: The Permanent Collection – MAQS*	$9.95
3793	*Quilts: The Permanent Collection – MAQS Volume II*	$9.95
3789	**Roots, Feathers & Blooms**, Linda Giesler Carlson	$16.95
4512	**Sampler Quilt Blocks from Native American Designs**, Dr. Joyce Mori	$14.95
3796	**Seasons of the Heart & Home: Quilts for a Winter's Day**, Jan Patek	$18.95
3761	**Seasons of the Heart & Home: Quilts for Summer Days**, Jan Patek	$18.95
2357	**Sensational Scrap Quilts**, Darra Duffy Williamson	$24.95
4783	**Silk Ribbons by Machine**, Jeanie Sexton	$15.95
3929	**The Stori Book of Embellishing**, Mary Stori	$16.95
3903	**Straight Stitch Machine Appliqué**, Letty Martin	$16.95
3792	**Striplate Piecing**, Debra Wagner	$24.95
3930	**Tessellations & Variations**, Barbara Ann Caron	$14.95
3788	**Three-Dimensional Appliqué**, Anita Shackelford	$24.95
4596	**Ties, Ties, Ties: Traditional Quilts from Neckties**, Janet B. Elwin	$19.95
3931	**Time-Span Quilts: New Quilts from Old Tops**, Becky Herdle	$16.95
4919	**Transforming Fabric**, Carolyn Dahl	$29.95
2029	**A Treasury of Quilting Designs**, Linda Goodmon Emery	$14.95
3847	**Tricks with Chintz**, Nancy S. Breland	$14.95
2286	**Wonderful Wearables: A Celebration of Creative Clothing**, Virginia Avery	$24.95
4812	**Who's Who in American Quilting**, edited by Bonnie Browning **(HB)**	$49.95
4956	**Variegreat! New Dimensions in Traditional Quilts**, Linda Glantz	$19.95
4972	**20th Century Quilts**, Cuesta Benberry and Joyce Gross	$9.95